Welcome To Colonial Williamsburg

A visit to Colonial Williamsburg is a rendezvous with an important chapter of America's history and with an entire community that existed two centuries ago. The experience includes encounters with the great deeds of patriot leaders as well as with the daily activities of the less well known people who also lived in eighteenth-century Williamsburg. The result is a new awareness of and kinship with the men, women, and children of early America. Much of the thinking and action that led to the creation of our nation took place in eighteenth-century Williamsburg. For example, the Virginia Declaration of Rights, written by George Mason, was the basis for the first ten amendments to the U. S. Constitution.

People from all walks of life created the Virginia colony, and here in Williamsburg a visitor sees their public buildings, craft shops, stores, townhouses, and homes of the "middling sort." Gentry, planters, merchants, free blacks, servants free and slave, travelers, and foreign visitors all congregated in the colony's capital. Public ordinances assured a well fenced, orderly landscape of public grounds, private gardens, and graceful vistas.

Buildings, gardens, and other physical reminders of the past cannot convey fully the meaning of early Williamsburg, however. The history programs at Colonial Williamsburg help visitors discover the past by bringing to life the homes, cares, accomplishments, and failures of residents in and travelers to Virginia's colonial capital. Colonial Williamsburg strives to provide present visitors with an experience that is enjoyable, educational, and relevant to their lives today.

Our visitors provide the single largest source of financial support for Colonial Williamsburg's museum and educational programs by their purchase of admission tickets. The balance of the annual cost of preserving and maintaining the Historic Area and of presenting the educational programs of the Colonial Williamsburg Foundation to the public is derived from charitable contributions from generous friends, sales of craft objects, reproductions, and educational materials, revenues from hotel and restaurant operations, income from rental properties, and income from an endowment fund.

All of us at Colonial Williamsburg appreciate the many ways in which you support our programs and purposes. Your participation is essential to the long-term future of the organization and all it has come to mean to millions of Americans and friends from abroad.

CHARLES R. LONGSWORTH, *President*
The Colonial Williamsburg Foundation

The Capitol.

Official Guide to

Colonial Williamsburg

Text by Michael Olmert

with

Drawings of Buildings by Peter C. Turner
Maps by Louis Luedtke and Design by Richard Stinely

The Colonial Williamsburg Foundation
Williamsburg, Virginia

Library of Congress Cataloging in Publication Data
Olmert, Michael.
Official guide to Colonial Williamsburg.
Includes index.
1. Williamsburg (Va.)—Description—Guide-books. I. Title.
F234.W7046   1985   917.55′42520443   85-3729

ISBN 0-87935-111-X

Printed in the United States of America

Contents

Your Visit To Williamsburg

A VISIT to Williamsburg is a journey into America's past. Here, in the restored capital of eighteenth-century Virginia and at neighboring Carter's Grove plantation, you will enter the day-to-day world of men and women long since passed from the scene. Nevertheless, their lives shaped the world we inhabit today in both common and extraordinary ways.

We urge you to begin your visit at the Visitor Center. There you may plan your tour of the Historic Area, buy admission tickets, and make reservations for dining, overnight accommodations, and evening events and special programs. You should also view *Williamsburg—The Story of a Patriot*, a classic thirty-five-minute film that brings the story of the American Revolution in Virginia dramatically to life.

Your admission ticket entitles you to use the bus system operated by Colonial Williamsburg, which serves the Historic Area and the Visitor Center–Motor House complex. The bus will take you to the Historic Area and to your encounter with history.

You will need a guide for your journey in space and time at Colonial Williamsburg. This book is designed to be that companion.

The orientation map on the next page shows the entire Historic Area with its principal streets, major landmarks, and eight geographical areas.

This guide to the Historic Area of Williamsburg is divided into eight sections. Each section contains attractions that require an admission ticket. A 🎫 indicates that you will need a ticket to see the attraction.

The text of each section tells the history of a particular area of the town and, along with a detailed map of the area, drawings of buildings, and information about exhibition sites, historical personages, stores, and visitor services, illuminates that area's physical and historical landscape.

The symbol ♿ indicates that a facility is accessible to the handicapped.

Each area map's symbols will enable you to identify and locate the following items:

- Historic Area
- Attractions that require an admission ticket
- Places to shop
- Places to dine
- Exhibition gardens
- Places to buy tickets and get information
- Rest rooms
- Cold drinks
- Water fountains
- Other services and places to visit

Character sketches based on real people that combine fact and conjecture appear in each section.

Each section of the Historic Area may be toured independently and in any order.

Duke of Gloucester Street.

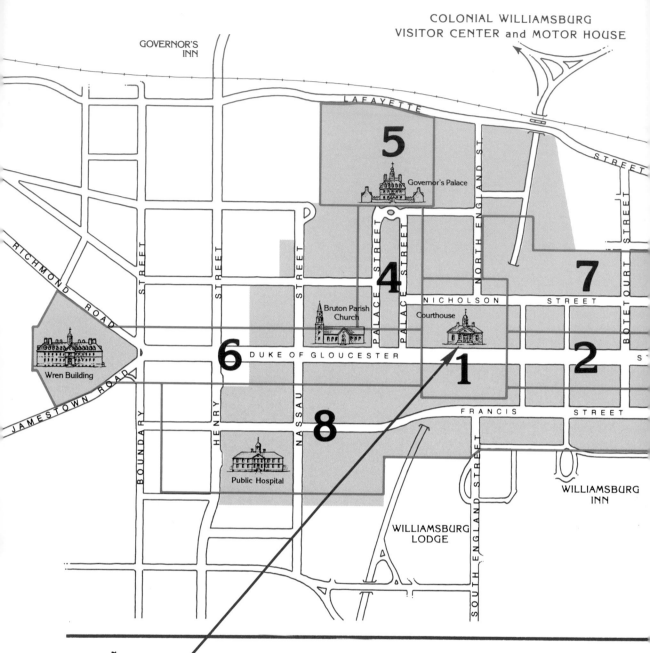

START YOUR TOUR of the Historic Area at the **Courthouse** on **Market Square.** This landmark building, which is readily identified when approached from bus stop 1 or when entering the Historic Area from the Williamsburg Inn and Lodge or from Merchants Square, will orient you for your tour of the Market Square area and to tour the rest of restored Williamsburg.

Other landmark buildings, to which you can orient yourself when you tour other areas of the town, are the **Capitol,** east or "downtown" on Duke of Gloucester Street from the Courthouse, and **Bruton Parish Church,** the **Governor's Palace,** and the **Wren Building** at the College of William and Mary, which are west or "uptown" on Duke of Gloucester Street. Nicholson Street and Francis Street are parallel to Duke of Gloucester Street on the north

**The Historic Area is divided into the
following eight geographical areas:**

**The following buildings serve as
orientation landmarks:**

WALLER STREET

Capitol

LOOKING NORTH

CAPITOL

COURTHOUSE

BRUTON PARISH
CHURCH

GOVERNOR'S
PALACE

WREN BUILDING

PUBLIC HOSPITAL

and south respectively. In colonial times they were often called simply "back streets." The *Public Hospital* is located just south of Francis Street. Each area of the town has its corresponding section in this guidebook.

When you have finished you should be acquainted with the eighteenth-century community of Williamsburg and with some of the people, events, and characteristics that made it significant in the early history of our nation. Between the covers of this guidebook, in the histories of its people and places, is the story of a town that shaped and was shaped by many of the events and personalities that made a new people and a new nation out of England's American colonies. We hope you will keep referring to this guidebook after your journey to Williamsburg and by this means continue learning from the story it tells.

WILLIAMSBURG . . . is regularly laid out in parallel streets, intersected by others at right angles; has a handsome square in the center, through which runs the principal street, one of the most spacious in North-America, three quarters of a mile in length, and above a hundred feet wide. At the ends of this street are two public buildings, the college and the capitol: and although the houses are of wood, covered with shingles, and but indifferently built, the whole makes a handsome appearance.

—THE REVEREND ANDREW BURNABY, who came to Virginia from England in 1759 and remained until 1760, described Williamsburg in his *Travels through the Middle Settlements in North-America, in the Years 1759 and 1760.*

The City of Williamsburg

Jamestown, the Seventeenth-Century Capital

THE story of Williamsburg, the capital of eighteenth-century Virginia, really began at seventeenth-century Jamestown. For over ninety years after the first English adventurers set foot on Virginia soil, Jamestown served as the seat of government and administrative center of England's largest colony in North America. From its statehouse on the banks of the James River, officials and lawmakers governed the colonists, promoted the spread of settlement, and, less honorably, established a system of slavery. As Virginia grew, Jamestown did not. And after nearly a century, it was clear that it would not.

Located on a low, swampy island, Jamestown had earned a notorious reputation as a disease-ridden, indefensible settlement. Furthermore, by the late seventeenth century the scraggly little village no longer projected an image befitting a wealthy American colony. When the statehouse burned for the fourth time in 1698, many Virginians, including the royal governor, Francis Nicholson, seized upon the accident as an opportunity to move the capital. Several prospective sites were considered. After some debate, members of the House of Burgesses chose an area of high ground between the York and James rivers five miles from the old capital city, a site known as Middle Plantation.

Middle Plantation had been founded in the early seventeenth century as an outpost to defend against Indian attacks. By 1690 it had developed into a small village of widely scattered houses that also contained a church, several stores, a tavern, two mills, and, after 1695, the College of William and Mary. Several of Virginia's leading politicians lived near Middle Plantation. On several occasions, most notably during Bacon's Rebellion in 1676 and 1677 when Jamestown was burned to the ground, Middle Plantation served as a substitute capital. Its main attractions as a potential site for the capital were several. First, it was located on high ground between two rivers and therefore was relatively mosquito and disease free. Its inland location was thought to be safe from naval bombardment, and it was the home of the College, one of Virginia's principal institutions. Finally, and perhaps most importantly, as a relatively undeveloped area Middle Plantation provided an essentially blank slate upon which an appropriate capital city could be planned and built unhindered by previous building. Begun in 1699, the new city was named Williamsburg in honor of the king of England, William III.

Williamsburg's Town Plan and Landmarks

Once the decision was made to move the capital from Jamestown to Middle Plantation, the small village there was not al-

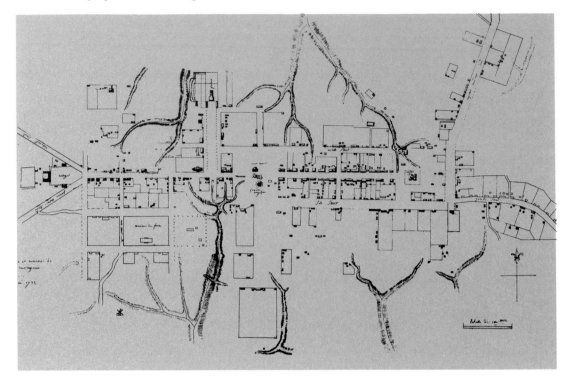

The Frenchman's Map, probably drawn by a French officer for the purpose of billeting troops after the siege of Yorktown in 1781, shows the streets and many of the buildings of eighteenth-century Williamsburg.

lowed to grow naturally to accommodate the colonial government. Instead, an entirely new capital city was imposed on the site. The desire to design a completely new city complemented one of the motives for moving the capital from Jamestown. Many Virginians thought their colony was becoming too important to be served by anything less than a capital city built to reflect Virginia's preeminence among England's American colonies. In all probability, Governor Nicholson took the initiative for the new design. He had successfully planned Annapolis when he was governor of Maryland, and he was well versed in the latest principles of urban planning. The town plan of Williamsburg reflected those principles. The fact that it was newly built in the Virginia countryside, following a predetermined design, is a key to discovering in restored Williamsburg traces of the eighteenth-century city. Several important physical landmarks were central to Nicholson's plan and are still extant.

The first of these is a large open area in the center of the town known as Market Square. Today you will find the Powder Magazine, built on Governor Alexander Spotswood's orders in 1715, and the Courthouse on Market Square. In the eighteenth century the square served as a town common where markets and fairs were held regularly. Another distinctive feature of the colonial capital that is still present today crosses the square in an east-west direction. Duke of Gloucester Street, or "the Main Street" as it was known in the eighteenth century, extends "uptown" from the College of William and Mary at the western end "downtown" to the Capitol building at the eastern. Designed to be ninety-nine feet wide and nearly one mile long, this street was a broad, open avenue that highlighted the linear aspects of the city plan.

To the west of Market Square, the city was laid out in the shape of a square centered on Bruton Parish Church. The first church building, completed by 1683, stood a little to the north of the present structure, which replaced it in 1715. The fact that a church was already standing here is one of the main reasons the design of this section of town is as it is. Farther to the west is the main College building, called the Wren Building in honor of Sir Christopher Wren, an important seventeenth-century English architect who was reputed to have inspired its design. Located just outside the eighteenth-century city boundary, the College building was the key visual element at the west end of Duke of Gloucester Street. The symbolic importance of this part of Williamsburg with its religious and educational institutions was and still is reinforced by the Governor's Palace. By its location at the head of a wide green avenue running north from the church, this landmark was meant to command an eighteenth-century visitor's attention— as it still does that of modern visitors.

If you walk east from Market Square, you will be drawn to the dominant landmark designed for that end of town— the Capitol. To help focus attention on this most important building, the eastern end of Williamsburg was framed by two back streets, Nicholson on the north and Francis on the south.

The New Towns of the Eighteenth Century

People's early expectations for Williamsburg were inspired by an older vision of what cities could accomplish. Traditionally they were viewed as centers of learning, religion, and government. As you walk along Williamsburg's main street, you can see that the city planners anchored the town on the College, church, and Capitol, the physical symbols of a traditional city. An eighteenth-century visitor to Williams-

burg when it was still little more than a grid of vacant lots would have known from these three official buildings that he was in a capital city. But even as Williamsburg began to grow, this older understanding of what a city was meant to be was being supplanted by a newer vision.

In England, in her overseas colonies, and throughout western Europe a people who once were content to acquire relatively few material possessions began to demand more—more clothes, more fabrics, more furniture, more books. This surge in consumer demand transformed villages and towns into something that not even great metropolitan cities like London

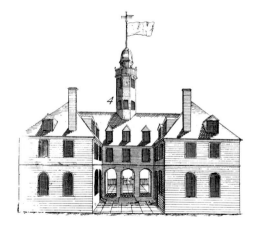

The "Bodleian Plate," an engraved copperplate of about 1740, was discovered at Oxford University. Renderings of the Capitol (above) and the Governor's Palace assisted in the reconstruction of those buildings.

had been before. Some grew into manufacturing centers, making the goods that consumers increasingly began to demand. Others became retail centers selling affordable goods to regional markets of ordinary buyers.

The impact of this shift toward commerce-centered activities was even felt in far-off Virginia. By the mid-eighteenth century Williamsburg had taken on a more modern look. Retail stores with display windows filled with merchandise for almost every man's and woman's pocket lined the streets. Artisans like silversmiths and blacksmiths frequently sold imported goods in their shops. Amidst the business of government, Williamsburg catered to a growing number of eager new consumers. Because there is much that you will recognize of our own world here, restored Williamsburg is a bridge to that time when the consumer age was just beginning.

The Williamsburg Community

Unlike Jamestown, Williamsburg did not remain a small, undeveloped administrative center. Partly because the colony's growth continued throughout the eighteenth century and partly because eco-

nomic forces reshaped Virginia society, Williamsburg fulfilled the expectation of its founders and kept pace with the growing colony.

At first the business of government attracted the nucleus of Williamsburg's urban population. Joining the small staff already living at the College were the governor, his household, and the clerks of various government offices. Soon the regular meetings of the General Court, the attendance of councillors on the governor, and the periodic meetings of the General Assembly brought a number of other people to Williamsburg to support these governmental activities. Taverns were established to feed and house those in town on government business. Lawyers settled here to be close to the General Court. As the century progressed, more and more stores were opened to provide merchandise to out-of-town shoppers. The townspeople engaged in these activities needed to be housed and provided with foodstuffs that they didn't grow themselves. Carpenters and masons moved to town to build houses and shops. Bakers, tailors, and barbers settled here to serve both visitors and townspeople. Much of the heavy and domestic work around town was performed by

The Powder Magazine was erected in 1715. After the Revolution it saw use as a market, a Baptist meetinghouse, a dancing school, and a livery stable.

The Prentis Store is Williamsburg's best surviving example of a colonial store. Built in 1739–1740, it survived into the twentieth century as a gas station.

blacks, most of them slaves, although a few were free. By the eve of the American Revolution nearly two thousand men, women, and children—roughly half white, half black—lived in the capital city.

Together these men and women formed a complex community, which is still possible for you to see in the social landscape they created within the town plan of Governor Nicholson's design. As you walk toward the Capitol from Market Square, for example, the increasing diversity of artisans' shops, stores, taverns, and houses crowding in on the Capitol gives the correct impression that this was the busiest section of town. The townspeople who lived and worked here competed for the business of visitors to the Capitol. A different landscape can be seen around the Courthouse. As you look north and south, several large, elegant townhouses meet the eye as they would have in the late eighteenth century. The clamor of marketplace vendors notwithstanding, the open space of Market Square had a special appeal for the prominent men who built these imposing dwellings. It provided an attractive vista for their homes. After mid-century the long, open avenue in front of the Governor's Palace had a similar attraction. Earlier it had contained a mixture of small houses, busy shops, and a theater. Even after the large houses came to be built, the working character of the Palace green persisted here and there.

As you walk past Bruton Parish Church toward the College, you can still glimpse several small open fields that gave something of a pastoral air to the west end of Williamsburg in the eighteenth century. A few stores, artisans' shops, and taverns line the streets here, but from a businessman's point of view this end of town was not as desirable as downtown near the Capitol. It was common for townspeople living here to buy half-acre lots in blocks of two or more, which they turned into small urban estates. Both ornamental and practical gardens filled much of the open space and reinforced the residential character that Nicholson intended for this part of the capital. The back streets of Williamsburg—Prince George, Scotland, Ireland, and especially Francis and Nicholson streets as they extended to the east—strengthened this countrified aspect of the town. Busy shops commonly adjoined or faced large urban estates along the north and south edges of Williamsburg. In the eighteenth century the line between town and country was blurred. People living along these streets often commented on the pleasant location of their homes.

An eighteenth-century traveler in the city would have experienced some of the same sensations that the restored city offers modern visitors. He would have encountered the hustle and bustle of shops, taverns, and stores. He would have glimpsed open vistas and pleasing views. He would have heard the voices of people working, the ringing of bells at the College, church, and Capitol, and the rattle of carriages and wagons moving along the streets. Williamsburg in the eighteenth century was a community—alive and vibrant—something that you too can conjure up in your imagination as you tour the city today.

Williamsburg after the War

For eighty years Williamsburg was Virginia's capital. Although it grew into a far more impressive urban community than had Jamestown, not all eighteenth-century Virginians were happy that the capital was located here. Several times Williamsburg supporters had to beat back efforts to move the capital someplace else. But in 1780, for reasons similar to those offered in 1699—military defense, healthier climate, and a more central location—proponents of a new capital prevailed. The capital of Revolutionary Virginia removed to Richmond where it remains today.

Despite the loss of the capital, Williamsburg did not die as Jamestown had. It continued to be a county seat, and it continued to house two important institutions—the College of William and Mary and the Public Hospital for the insane. Throughout the nineteenth century Williamsburg served as an important market center for nearby farmers and their families. As a quiet college and market town, it witnessed the Civil War firsthand, experienced the emancipation of slaves, and welcomed the railroad in the 1880s. Although fires occasionally raged in parts of the old city, Williamsburg was spared major destruction. Old eighteenth-century homes were repaired, renovated, and continued in use until the twentieth century.

The Reverend W. A. R. Goodwin, rector of Bruton Parish in the opening years of the twentieth century, was inspired by the survival of so many eighteenth-century buildings and by the role Williamsburg played during the American Revolution. He dreamed of restoring the city to its

The John Crump House before and after reconstruction.

Dr. W. A. R. Goodwin (left), who dreamed of restoring eighteenth-century Williamsburg, and Mr. John D. Rockefeller, Jr., who made the dream a reality.

eighteenth-century glory. Goodwin was able to communicate the power of his vision to John D. Rockefeller, Jr., in 1926. With Rockefeller's involvement the city's restoration was undertaken. Original eighteenth-century sites were acquired and their buildings carefully returned to their colonial appearance. Nineteenth- and twentieth-century houses and buildings were removed and in their places carefully researched reconstructions arose on original eighteenth-century foundations. John D. Rockefeller, Jr., gave the project his enthusiastic support for more than thirty years. He contributed the necessary funds to accomplish the restoration and established an endowment to provide for its educational programs.

Today the Historic Area of Williamsburg is both a museum and a living city. Many of the restored and reconstructed homes and outbuildings are residences for Colonial Williamsburg's employees. The Historic Area is also the heart of a larger modern city of about ten thousand residents, which in turn serves a metropolitan area of approximately thirty thousand people. Colonial Williamsburg is operated by the Colonial Williamsburg Foundation, a nonprofit educational organization. Today the city is administered by a mayor, council, and city manager.

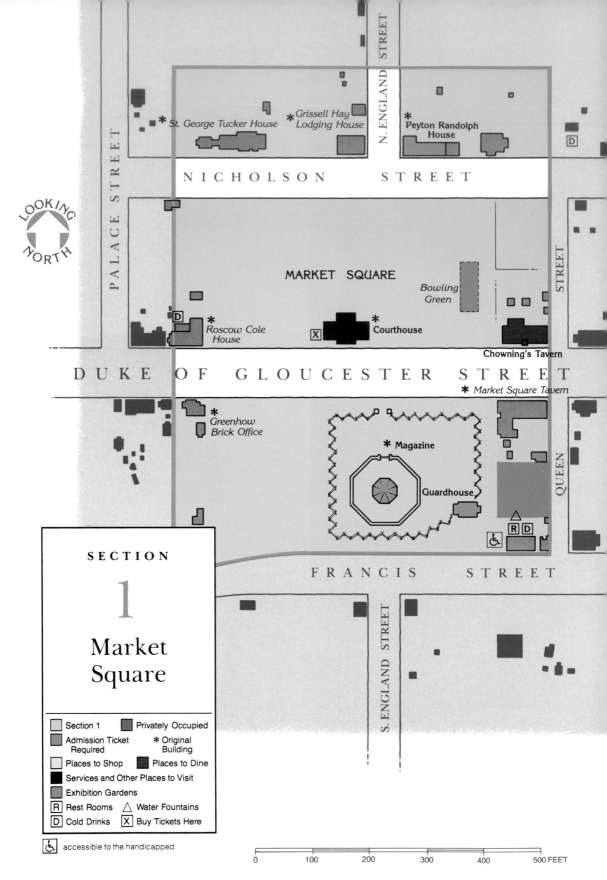

LOOKING NORTH

ST. GEORGE TUCKER HOUSE
* St. George Tucker House
* Grissell Hay Lodging House
* Peyton Randolph House

N. ENGLAND STREET

PALACE STREET

NICHOLSON STREET

D

MARKET SQUARE

Bowling Green

STREET

D
* Roscow Cole House
X Courthouse

Chowning's Tavern

DUKE OF GLOUCESTER STREET

* Market Square Tavern

* Greenhow Brick Office

* Magazine

Guardhouse

QUEEN

R D

FRANCIS STREET

S. ENGLAND STREET

SECTION

1

Market
Square

Section 1
Admission Ticket Required
Places to Shop
Services and Other Places to Visit
Exhibition Gardens
R Rest Rooms
D Cold Drinks

Privately Occupied
* Original Building
Places to Dine

△ Water Fountains
X Buy Tickets Here

accessible to the handicapped.

0   100   200   300   400   500 FEET

18

Market Square

MARKET SQUARE, a green open space about halfway between the College and the Capitol, was set aside as a permanent area for markets and fairs by an act of the General Assembly early in the eighteenth century.

There, before dawn on each market day—as often as six times a week later in the century—the town slowly came alive. People from nearby farms brought their produce to town in creaking wagons or carts. Sometimes cattle and sheep competed for road space leading to the square, driven on by shouting children and yelping dogs. In the pre-dawn light, vendors unloaded meat, eggs, milk, butter, fish, crabs, oysters, fruit, vegetables, and other provender, displaying their wares on makeshift counters of pine boards.

Armed with lists of the provisions needed for the day, housewives, cooks, and kitchen slaves selected the freshest eggs, the ripest peaches, the choicest cuts of meat. Shopping was a daily chore in an age without refrigeration.

By mid-morning most of the produce had been sold or looked shopworn. The crowds began to melt away. Some of the farmers repaired to one of the taverns conveniently located next to the square to relax, listen to the local gossip, and quench their thirst.

The Williamsburg charter of 1722 established two fairs each year, one on April 23, the feast of St. George, the patron saint of England, and the other on December 12. A variety of merchandise, including livestock, was sold on the square. People enjoyed games, puppet shows, horse races, cockfights, dancing and fiddling for prizes, and a chase for a "Pig, with the Tail soap'd."

Auctions of slaves, goods, and land occurred on Market Square. After Josiah Chowning's death in 1772, for example, some property that he owned and one of his slaves were auctioned off in front of the Courthouse—within sight of the tavern that bears his name.

Market Square was also important as a seat of local government. In 1715, the courthouse for James City County fronted on Market Square. The present structure, built at the center of the square in 1770, housed both the municipal and the county courts until 1932. In all, a local government building stood on or adjacent to the square for more than two hundred years.

Near the Courthouse was the training field for the Williamsburg Militia Company, which mustered there several times a year. With a few exceptions, the colonial militia consisted of every free, white, able-bodied man, aged sixteen to sixty, who was a British subject. A militia muster brought together members of different social classes without leveling social distinctions. Musters formalized and validated the authority figures in colonial society, the large landowners who were appointed to command the militia and who served without pay. Those officers deemed military service both an honor and an obligation, and they could be fined as much as twenty pounds for failure to perform. By contrast, three shillings was the typical fine for an absent militiaman.

Much of the rest of the local population turned out to watch the training and drills in quick loading and shooting. All was not marching and manual-of-arms practice, however. Militiamen participated in foot races, wrestling matches, and cudgeling standoffs, with prizes being awarded to the victors. Afterward, the officers might treat the entire company to a hogshead of rum punch.

Market Square's central location made it

Meet . . .
Martha Cripps

Martha Cripps, a hardworking woman, cared for her family and managed a plantation as well. Martha illustrates the tenuous and fragile nature of marriage in colonial Virginia because of the high death rate. Only thirty-four in 1740, she was a widow for the third time, Thomas Cripps, her last husband, having died four years before. Martha had had children by each of her husbands. John and Mary Bryan were about fourteen and twelve, Rebecka Frayser was about nine, and John, her youngest, was nearly six. The family lived on a small plantation (as farms were called in the eighteenth century) about an hour's cart ride from Williamsburg.

Like most of her rural neighbors, Martha raised livestock and cash crops such as corn and tobacco with the help of her older son and an adult slave named Sam. Because she lived close to Williamsburg, Martha also sold produce—milk and butter throughout the year, fruits and vegetables seasonally—at the town's market.

Market days were especially busy for Martha. Rising before sunup, she put John, Sam, and Bess, her slave woman, to their daily tasks, packed the produce for sale in the cart, drove to Williamsburg, and set up her stand. She needed to be prompt because her goods brought the highest prices early in the morning when customers were the most plentiful. Nor did Martha idle away the rest of the morning. Between customers she carded wool to be spun into yarn later. Martha also had time to worry about problems at home. Bess was old and growing feeble. Unless the younger children helped, Bess usually was unable to finish preparations for the family's midday dinner.

By late morning Martha was certain that she had sold all that she could, so she repacked the cart and returned home. There she continued her daily chores. Martha did the laundry, mended clothes, weeded the garden, checked on Sam and John in the field, and milked the cows. She ate a light supper as night fell, then finally went to bed. Thankful for being able to rest at the end of an exhausting day, her thoughts turned to the coming Sunday. Martha planned to attend church in Williamsburg. She looked forward to sharing the latest news and gossip with friends from her neighborhood after the service.

* *Courthouse*

a favorite place for public notices, official announcements, communal celebrations, and elections. In July 1746 a large bonfire was lit and the public consumed three barrels of punch in honor of the Duke of Cumberland's victory over Bonnie Prince Charlie at the battle of Culloden. On July 25, 1776, Benjamin Waller proclaimed the Declaration of Independence from the Courthouse steps to a huge throng after the news arrived from Philadelphia.

Elections were public affairs in colonial Virginia. Voters gathered in front of the Courthouse to choose the men who would serve as their representatives in the House of Burgesses.

Its convenient location must have been paramount in the decision to keep the town's fire engine, which was in use by 1756, on the square. Fire was a constant hazard in the eighteenth century. An efficient response to the threat of fire required organization and cooperation.

After the capital moved to Richmond in 1780, Market Square became the unrivaled civic center of Williamsburg. The prestige that a Market Square address conferred probably caused St. George Tucker to move a house from Palace Street to the square where it was enlarged to its present appearance. The Roscow Cole House, which might have been expected to front

Duke of Gloucester Street, was instead constructed in 1812 to face Market Square.

Market Square is dominated by the **Courthouse.** Like many other Virginia courthouses, it is T-shaped. Its formal design elements—round-headed windows, a cantilevered pediment, and an octagonal cupola with the original weather vane— add to and reinforce the official appearance of the building.

Two courts met regularly in the Courthouse, the James City County Court and the municipal court (known as the Hustings Court) for the city of Williamsburg. In colonial Virginia the county court was the principal agent of local government and exercised broad executive and judicial powers. Its criminal jurisdiction, however, was restricted to cases that did not involve life or limb. All cases involving slaves were tried before the county court. Serious crimes involving whites were heard by the General Court that met in the Capitol. The Hustings Court possessed the civil jurisdiction within the city that the James City County Court exercised in the adjacent county.

The Hustings Court met on the first Monday of each month, while the James City County Court convened on the second Monday. Sessions lasted several days until the backlog of cases was cleared.

Courthouse

Ticket not required

The Courthouse, an original building, serves as an orientation landmark. From the Courthouse, the Capitol is visible "down" Duke of Gloucester Street and Bruton Parish Church and the Wren Building at the College of William and Mary may be seen "up" the street. The Governor's Palace is located to the northwest. The Public Hospital is located just south of Francis Street between South Henry and Nassau streets.

Information, general admission tickets, and tickets for special tours and events are available at the Courthouse. All tours leave from the Courthouse.

The onlookers who often filled the courthouse to overflowing on court days got their fill of debtor and creditor tales, wife beaters, pig stealers, and more. The theatricality of the proceedings was heightened because convicted offenders were usually punished immediately after the verdict. Often this meant public flogging at the whipping post conveniently located just outside the courthouse. Other convicts were locked in the stocks or pillory where they were exposed to public ridicule and abuse.

The *Magazine* was erected in 1715 after Lieutenant Governor Alexander Spotswood urgently requested a "good substantial house of brick" in which to store the arms and ammunition dispatched from London for the defense of the colony. Governor Spotswood himself is credited with the Magazine's unusual octagonal design.

The Magazine assumed added importance during the French and Indian War, 1754–1763, when for the first time the colony supported large-scale military operations in the Ohio Valley, territory that the crown claimed under the Virginia charter of 1609. Because the amount of gunpowder in storage exceeded sixty thousand pounds, the residents of Williamsburg felt that the Magazine needed further protec-

Guardhouse 🇹   *Magazine* 🇹

Magazine and Guardhouse

The octagonal Magazine, an original building, served as the arsenal for the Virginia colony. Authentic firearms and military equipment are exhibited here. Muskets are fired year-round, and visitors may see such seasonal activities as cannon firing and bullet casting, as well as soldiers cooking outside, stitching tents, and painting cannon carriages.

A replica of a 1750 Newsham patent fire engine is housed in a lean-to on the west wall of the Guardhouse. It takes as many as eighteen men to operate the fire engine, which is demonstrated during warm weather on the streets of the town.

tion. A high wall was therefore built around the Magazine and a *Guardhouse* was constructed nearby.

At its busiest, the Magazine probably contained two to three thousand Brown Bess muskets and enough shot, powder, and flints to equip a formidable army. Other military equipment—tents, tools, swords, pikes, canteens, and cooking utensils—was also stored in the Magazine.

During the night of April 20–21, 1775, the Magazine played a dramatic role in an incident that did much to precipitate the Revolution in Virginia. Governor Dunmore ordered British marines under cover of darkness to remove the gunpowder which was stored in the Magazine. Dunmore's act was a reprisal against the Second Virginia Convention for passing an act to assemble and train the militia.

Public indignation rose to fever pitch. Troops were mustered.

Patrick Henry led a group of armed volunteers from faraway Hanover County toward the capital, demanding the return of the powder or payment for it. Governor Dunmore, heeding the counsel of town leaders, backed down, payment was made, and the "rebels" dispersed. An uneasy quiet prevailed until news of the battles at Lexington and Concord on April 19 reached Williamsburg a few days later.

After the Revolution an arsenal at Williamsburg was no longer needed, although the Confederate forces did store powder in the Magazine during the Civil War. The building was later used as a market, a Baptist meetinghouse, a dancing school, and finally as a livery stable.

The Association for the Preservation of Virginia Antiquities made the safeguarding of the Magazine its first project. In 1986 Colonial Williamsburg obtained the Magazine from the A.P.V.A.

*   *Greenhow Brick Office*

Directly west of the Magazine is the **Greenhow Brick Office.** Although Williamsburg was the port of entry for the upper James River, there was no customhouse in town, a situation much belabored by the inspector general of customs when he visited in 1760. Accounts indicate that a public building, located "in the square" on municipal property, existed by 1764. It is likely that this modest brick structure was used as the Williamsburg customhouse.

The brick portion of the **Roscow Cole House** was erected in 1812 to face Market Square by Roscow Cole, a local merchant. The westerly wooden frame section is a reconstruction of an eighteenth-century building. An 1830 insurance policy called this structure a dry goods store.

The **St. George Tucker House** is one of the most admired residences in Williamsburg. It belonged to noted jurist St. George Tucker, who attended William and Mary where he later became professor of law.

Tucker bought the property in 1788 and moved an older building, which had faced Palace Green, to this site. After the capital moved to Richmond and the Governor's Palace burned down, the focus of town life shifted to Market Square. Tucker naturally preferred to orient his house toward the center of Williamsburg.

Tucker enlarged the house several times to accommodate his growing family. Today the exterior has been painted in the same colors—"Spanish brown, pure White, Chocolate, dark brick, yellow Ochre, straw-colour, and pale Stone colour"—that Tucker specified in an agreement drawn up in 1798 with a local painter.

The **Grissell Hay Lodging House** to the east is on the site of one of the first houses on Market Square, which belonged to Dr. Archibald Blair, a Scotch physician and a partner in Williamsburg's leading mercantile business, the Prentis Store. The present house probably dates from the mid-

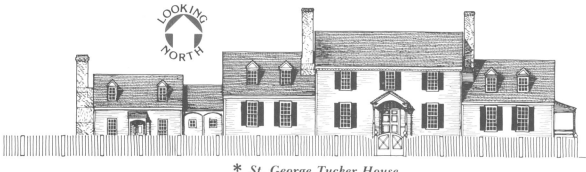

*   *St. George Tucker House*

* *Roscow Cole House*

Meet . . . St. George Tucker

St. George Tucker came to Virginia from Port Royal, Bermuda, in 1771 to enter the College of William and Mary. He then read law under George Wythe, whom he succeeded as professor of law at the College in 1790. Known as the "American Blackstone" because of his annotated edition of the celebrated *Commentaries*, Tucker was a judge of the United States District Court at the time of his death in 1827.

Tucker's habit of keeping almost everything he wrote proved useful to preservationists, who have painted his house in colors specified in Tucker's 1798 agreement with Jeremiah Satterwhite, a local painter. It also enables historians to reconstruct neighborhood connections. For example, Tucker had standing accounts with local merchants, including John Greenhow and, later, Greenhow's son Robert. Tucker gave his wife a regular allowance for household expenses. After several years in the 1790s during which he incurred large medical bills, Tucker agreed to pay local doctors Galt and Barraud an annual stipend to attend his family, which included not only his immediate relations but his house servants as well.

In addition to his professional accomplishments, St. George Tucker was a poet and essayist, an amateur astronomer, an inventor, and an avid gardener. His writings describe the town belles of his student days, tell of Christmas celebrations and wedding festivities, depict domestic gatherings at his fireside, honor or poke fun at his friends and neighbors, and satirize the legal profession.

Tucker often wrote about his house and garden on Market Square. He liked living in Williamsburg and was quick to defend the town even though he realized that its days of glory had ended in 1780. "Few villages can boast a more pleasant situation," he wrote in 1795, "more respectable inhabitants, or a more agreeable and friendly society."

* *Grissell Hay Lodging House*

* *Peyton Randolph House* ▣

eighteenth century. Apothecary Peter Hay, whose shop on Duke of Gloucester Street burned in 1756, lived here in the 1760s. After Hay's death, his widow, Grissell, operated the dwelling as a lodging house. Keeping lodging houses (the equivalents of today's guest homes) was an occupation often engaged in by widows who needed to support themselves and their children.

The white frame *Peyton Randolph House* at the corner of Nicholson and North England streets was the home of one of the most prominent families in colonial Virginia.

The house has three parts. The oldest,

which originally faced west onto North England Street, was built about 1715. Sir John Randolph and his family were living there in 1724 when he bought the lot and the one and one-half story house next door. In the mid-eighteenth century the two were linked by a two-story central section that features a grand stairway and a monumental round-headed window. Inside the house is the best series of surviving paneled rooms in Williamsburg. Although most of the paneling is the usual yellow pine, the northeast room on the second floor of the oldest section is paneled completely in oak.

When he died in 1737, Sir John Ran-

Peyton Randolph House

▣

Home of the longtime speaker of the House of Burgesses and president of the first Continental Congress, the Peyton Randolph House is composed of three sections that were built between 1715 and mid-century. It served as a center for many social and political activities. In the house is the best series of original paneled rooms in Williamsburg. It is furnished with English and American antiques, including several pieces of Randolph family silver.

dolph willed the house to his widow during her lifetime and then to his son Peyton. Sir John also left his library to Peyton, "hoping he will betake himself to the study of law." Thomas Jefferson bought the library after his cousin Peyton's death in 1775. Jefferson's library later became the nucleus of the Library of Congress. A number of Randolph's books have been identified by signature or by bookplate among the Jefferson collection there.

Peyton fulfilled his father's hopes and studied law at the Inns of Court in London. He was appointed attorney general of the colony of Virginia in 1744, elected to the House of Burgesses in 1748, became

Peyton Randolph.

Meet . . . The Randolph Family

The Randolphs were the first family of Williamsburg during the colonial period. Considered the most distinguished lawyer in the colony, Sir John Randolph (1693–1737) was the only colonial-born Virginian to be honored with knighthood for his services to the crown.

Sir John's sons Peyton (1722–1775) and John (1727–1784) attended the College of William and Mary, trained at the Inns of Court, and then practiced law. Peyton became attorney general within a year of his return to Virginia after completing his legal training in England. John succeeded his brother in that post when Peyton was elected speaker of the House of Burgesses.

The Randolphs lived comfortably and married well. After their wedding in 1745, Peyton and his bride, Elizabeth Harrison of Berkeley plantation, resided in the house he inherited from his father. John and Ariana Randolph lived in Tazewell Hall, a handsome dwelling located at the southern end of South England Street. The John Randolphs entertained in style and their home became a popular literary and social center frequented by the town's and colony's elite, including the governors and their families.

Although both Peyton and John were political moderates who hoped for reconciliation with the mother country, they took opposing sides in the years before the American Revolution. From the mid-1760s John sided with the crown. He became a close friend of governors Fauquier and Botetourt and was a confidant of Governor Dunmore. Peyton supported the colonists' cause, presiding over sessions of the first and second Continental Congresses.

The war divided the Randolphs in another way. John and his wife and daughters sailed "home" to England in September 1775, but his son Edmund remained in America, serving as an aide-de-camp to General Washington.

Peyton Randolph died unexpectedly in Philadelphia of an apoplectic stroke in 1775. Embittered, John lived in England until his death in 1784, periodically petitioning Parliament to recoup the losses that he incurred when he left Virginia.

History has judged the Randolph brothers—one as a patriot leader, the other as "John the Tory."

Chowning's Tavern

speaker of the House in 1766, and presided over it at every session in the crucial decade before the Revolution. He was elected unanimously to be president of the first Continental Congress in 1774.

In August 1774, just before the Continental Congress convened, legislators met at the Peyton Randolph House to determine what course Virginia's delegates should follow. Thomas Jefferson was ill and could not attend, but he sent his suggestions to his cousin, Peyton, and they were read aloud to a group of patriots. Jefferson's document was soon printed and distributed as *A Summary View of the Rights of British America.* Too radical for some but moving to all, it was one of the influential tracts in leading colonial Americans toward independence.

Mrs. Betty Harrison Randolph continued to live in the house after her husband's death. She relinquished it for a time during the Revolution so that the Comte de Rochambeau could establish his headquarters in the building before the Yorktown campaign. General Lafayette visited the Peyton Randolph House when he came to Williamsburg in 1824.

Chowning's Tavern is located east of the Courthouse. In 1766 Josiah Chowning advertised the opening of his tavern "where all who please to favour me with their custom may depend on the best of entertainment for themselves, servants, and horses, and good pasturage."

Chowning's Tavern serves hearty fare similar to the dishes enjoyed by its patrons in the eighteenth century.

Across the street, **Market Square Tavern** has been a hostelry for more than two hundred years. Its most celebrated lodger was Thomas Jefferson, who rented rooms there from Thomas Craig, tailor, while he studied law under the guidance of George Wythe. Neither Chowning's nor Market Square Tavern, however, could compete with the more profitable establishments farther east down Duke of Gloucester Street toward the Capitol.

* *Market Square Tavern*

Dining Opportunities

CHOWNING'S TAVERN
(ticket not required)

Chowning's Tavern has been rebuilt to resemble an eighteenth-century alehouse. Chowning's served a less august clientele than the Raleigh or the King's Arms, so sturdy, country-made chairs and tables have been selected for today's furnishings.

Chowning's specialties include Brunswick stew, Welsh rabbit, oysters, clams, hearty sandwiches, and "Chowning's good Bread." "Gambols," with games, ballads, other entertainment, and light food and drink, occur every evening. When weather permits, guests are served in the garden behind the tavern, which is shaded by an arbor of scuppernong grapes.

American Express, Mastercard, and Visa credit cards are accepted.

"Gambols"—colonial games, music, entertainment, and various "diversions"—take place nightly at Josiah Chowning's Tavern.

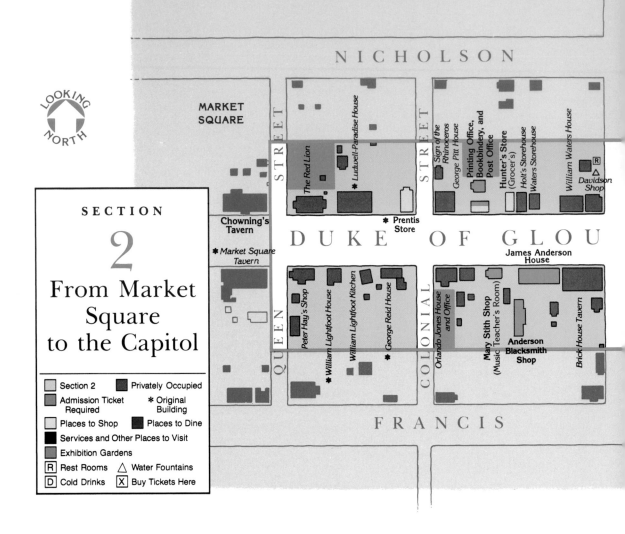

NICHOLSON STREET

MARKET SQUARE

LOOKING NORTH

The Red Lion

Ludwell-Paradise House

Sign of the Rhinoceros

George Pitt House

Printing Office, Bookbindery, and Post Office

Hunter's Store (Grocer's)

Holt's Storehouse

Waters Storehouse

William Waters House

Davidson Shop

Chowning's Tavern

* Prentis Store

* Market Square Tavern

DUKE OF GLOU

James Anderson House

QUEEN STREET

Peter Hay's Shop

* William Lightfoot House

William Lightfoot Kitchen

George Reid House

COLONIAL STREET

Orlando Jones House and Office

Mary Stith Shop (Music Teacher's Room)

Anderson Blacksmith Shop

Brick House Tavern

FRANCIS STREET

SECTION

2

From Market Square to the Capitol

- Section 2
- Admission Ticket Required
- Places to Shop
- Services and Other Places to Visit
- Exhibition Gardens
- R Rest Rooms
- D Cold Drinks
- Privately Occupied
- * Original Building
- Places to Dine
- △ Water Fountains
- X Buy Tickets Here

From Market Square to the Capitol

ATTRACTED by the numerous opportunities to eat, drink, or socialize, or perhaps to purchase the latest goods from London or a newspaper or book, most eighteenth-century townsfolk and visitors found their way "downtown" on Duke of Gloucester Street.

The three blocks of Duke of Gloucester Street from Market Square eastward to the Capitol were the busiest in eighteenth-century Williamsburg. General stores and specialty shops offered a wide range of goods at prices that ordinary consumers could afford. A number of taverns provided food, drink, and accommodations to an increasingly mobile and widely traveled public. In 1765 one visitor described the scene: "In the Day time people hurrying back and forwards from the Capitoll to the taverns, and at night, Carousing and Drinking in one Chamber and box and Dice in another, which Continues till morning."

Today these same blocks of Duke of Gloucester Street appear more neatly residential than they would have two hundred

30

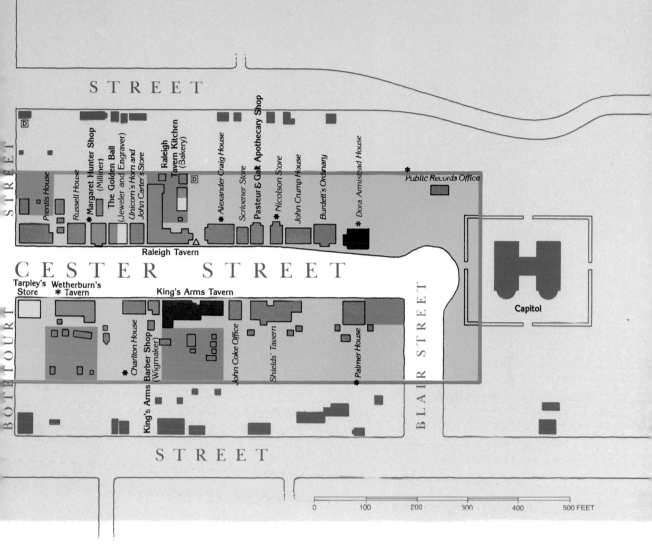

STREET

STREET

Prentis House

Russell House

Margaret Hunter Shop (Milliner)

The Golden Ball (Jeweler and Engraver)

Unicorn's Horn and John Carter's Store

Raleigh Tavern Kitchen (Bakery)

Alexander Craig House

Scrivener Store

Pasteur & Galt Apothecary Shop

Nicolson Store

John Crump House

Burdett's Ordinary

Dora Armistead House

Public Records Office

Raleigh Tavern

C E S T E R   S T R E E T

Tarpley's Store

Wetherburn's Tavern

King's Arms Tavern

Capitol

BOTETOURT

Charlton House

King's Arms Barber Shop (Wigmaker)

John Coke Office

Shields' Tavern

Palmer House

BLAIR STREET

STREET

0   100   200   300   400   500 FEET

years ago when many of the houses served interchangeably as shops, stores, taverns, and residences and the street bustled with mercantile activity. Lots at the end of the street nearest the Capitol had the most commercial character. They increased in value and often were subdivided as retailers and tavern keepers jostled for a lucrative location in this popular area.

William Parks, the first public printer in the colony of Virginia, began the weekly *Virginia Gazette* in 1736. Williamsburg thus became a communications center as news

of the world, of the colony, and of the city provided essential information to those whose affairs depended more and more on the "freshest advices" from far and near.

Light industry also developed at the back of the James Anderson property where Anderson established a blacksmithing operation. Anderson employed several smiths to man his seven forges. He served as public armorer of Virginia before and during the Revolutionary War, and he repaired arms for the American forces.

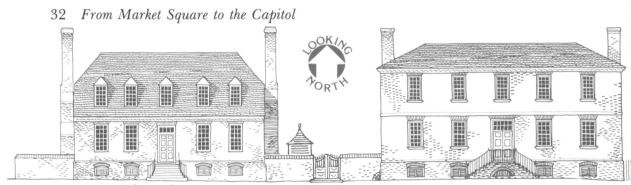

The Red Lion   * *Ludwell-Paradise House*

From Market Square to Colonial Street

This part of Duke of Gloucester Street was less commercially attractive than the east end because it was farther away from the hustle and bustle of people going to and from the Capitol. As a result, the block appears to have more open space, primarily because its half-acre lots were never subdivided. *The Red Lion* on the left suffered many failures and a rapid turnover of its tavern keepers, including Josiah Chowning at one time.

The haystack sign announces **Peter Hay's Shop.** Apothecary Hay fared somewhat better as a businessman than did his neighbors across the street until April 1756 when the *Maryland Gazette* reported that a fire broke out in his shop "and in less than Half an Hour entirely consumed the same, together with all Medicines, Utensils, &c." Fortunately "the Assistance of a Fire Engine" prevented damage to nearby buildings. A similar fire engine is now dis-

played and demonstrated near the Magazine Guardhouse in Market Square.

The **Ludwell-Paradise House,** one of the largest in town, is an example of the mixed use of buildings over time. Although an earlier structure existed on this site, the present dwelling probably was built by the Ludwell family as a townhouse about 1753. In Williamsburg, however, space meant money, and so even this elegant building was rented as a tenement for many years. Tavern keeper Joseph Pullet numbered Washington among his clients. Then William Rind—and later his widow, Clementina—operated a press on the premises.

The **William Lightfoot House and Kitchen** on the south side of the street belonged to a Yorktown merchant whose business apparently brought him to Williamsburg often enough so that he felt the need for a local dwelling.

The **George Reid House** next door may

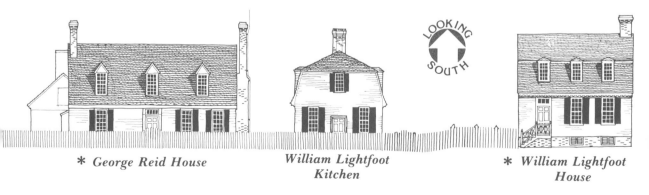

* *George Reid House*   *William Lightfoot Kitchen*   * *William Lightfoot House*

* *Prentis Store*

have been built as late as 1790 by a merchant who operated a store near the Capitol. Archaeological excavations revealed that a path near the house was paved with fragments of clay pipes that might have been broken in shipment to Williamsburg. Matching pieces have also been found at the Prentis Store across the street.

The ***Prentis Store*** is Williamsburg's best surviving example of a colonial store. The firm of Prentis and Company operated a highly successful general store in this handsome original building from 1740 until the Revolution. The tea shipment that Yorktown patriots threw into the York River during their tea party of 1774 was consigned to this firm.

A classic example of store architecture, its gable end faced the street. Through the door above, merchandise could easily be lifted into the loft. Windows along the sides were located toward the rear of the building to light the counting room and to leave long, blank walls for ample shelving in the sales area.

The Prentis Store dates from 1739–1740. It survived into the twentieth century as

Peter Hay's Shop

a gas station, which partially explains why so few changes were made to its fabric: it was likely considered "beneath" modernization or conversion. Prentis himself lived a block away in a substantial house at the corner of Botetourt and Duke of Gloucester streets, where he spent his leisure hours planning and planting a fine pleasure garden.

Goods representative of those sold in eighteenth-century stores are available at Prentis Store.

Meet . . . Clementina Rind

Clementina Rind (1740–1774) was the editor of the *Virginia Gazette* from 1773 to 1774. She also ran a public printing business and acted as publisher for the House of Burgesses, which meant that she was the first woman to operate such an enterprise in the colony. A widow, Clementina had five children. Her home and her printing business were both located in space she rented in the Ludwell-Paradise House.

Clementina came to Williamsburg from Annapolis, Maryland, with her husband, William. The Rinds established a second newspaper in Williamsburg. When William died in August 1773, Clementina assumed the editorship.

The result was a paper that closely followed her personal tastes. She printed news with a decided feminine slant. For example, when the governor's wife arrived in March 1774, Clementina published a personal poem emphasizing peace and contentment around Lord and Lady Dunmore's hearth instead of the usual formal address.

Clementina died of tuberculosis on September 25, 1774.

Sign of the Rhinoceros   ***George Pitt House***   ***Printing Office, Post Office,*** **and Bookbindery**   *Hunter's Store*

From Colonial Street to Botetourt Street

Although the ***George Pitt House*** was built as a residence, it sometimes served as a combination shop and dwelling in the eighteenth century. Sarah Packe, a young widow, had her millinery business here and also took in lodgers. Later Dr. George Pitt purchased the property and opened an apothecary shop, the ***Sign of the Rhinoceros.*** Dr. Pitt sold the property to printer John Dixon in 1774.

Next door, the ***Printing Office, Post Office, and Bookbindery*** was the town's communications hub. The box-like protruding windows decorated with the most recent prints from England not only proclaimed the latest fashions but helped to create a demand for them. Reading was recognized as an important element in commerce. The newspapers, broadsides, prints, magazines, novels, and inexpensive books on

Printing Office, Post Office, and Bookbindery

In these craft shops visitors watch newspapers, handbills, and books being printed on an eighteenth-century printing press. Bookbinding is also demonstrated. Type casting, wood-block cutting, and paper making and decorating are done in season.

Items typical of those sold at the colonial post office—books, prints, maps, stationery, seals and sealing wax, newspapers, games, and playing cards—are available at the Post Office.

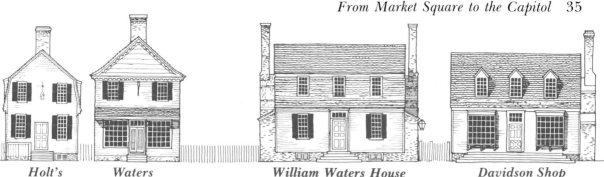

Holt's Storehouse   Waters Storehouse   **William Waters House**   Davidson Shop

every conceivable subject available here fueled the great information explosion of the eighteenth century.

William Parks published the *Virginia Gazette*, the first newspaper printed in the colony, from 1736 to 1750. He also became "public printer" to the General Assembly and the colony's first postmaster. Parks es-

Paper making is a seasonal craft.

tablished a paper mill just outside Williamsburg—"the first Mill of the Kind, that ever was erected in this Colony." In that venture he had the advice and backing of a fellow printer, Benjamin Franklin, who later purchased paper from Parks's mill.

Several hundred pieces of type, probably of Dutch origin, were unearthed at this site during archaeological excavations that also uncovered bookbinder's ornaments and crucibles in which Parks may have melted lead. The archaeologists also found lead border ornaments used in printing

paper money during the French and Indian War.

The next three structures—**Hunter's Store, Holt's Storehouse,** and **Waters Storehouse**—form a fine collection of reconstructed eighteenth-century commercial properties, all of which present their gable ends to the street.

Hunter's Store carries food products such as Virginia ham, jams and jellies, cider, tea, and coffee.

The three sugar loaves hanging outside Holt's Storehouse are the traditional sign of the grocer. In addition to groceries, John Holt sold dry goods and china.

Storekeepers tried to stock a wide range of products, especially yard goods and iron tools. Customers were hard to attract and harder to keep. One local merchant wrote to his Scottish supplier imploring him to send a variety of merchandise lest the shopkeeper lose the goodwill of his customers: "I find there will be an Absolute Necessity of allways [having] a good assortment in order to keep my Customers entirely to myself without allowing them to go to my neighbours for trifles."

The reconstructed **William Waters House** is named for its most prominent occupant, William Waters, a wealthy planter from the Eastern Shore, who bought it for his house in town when he moved to Williamsburg about 1750.

The **Davidson Shop** on the corner was once the apothecary shop of Robert Davidson, a "Practitioner in Physick" and mayor of Williamsburg in 1738.

Mary Stith Shop
(Music Teacher's Room)

Music lessons, rehearsals, and performances are presented in this small building. Students and teachers play instruments—recorders, harpsichords, violins—much like those on which Virginians performed two hundred years ago.

Orlando Jones, born in 1681, owned the original **Orlando Jones House and Office** on the south side of the street. His granddaughter Martha married George Washington. The garden is open to the public.

Mary Stith, daughter of William Stith, president of the College of William and Mary from 1752 to 1755, owned the small structure that is known as the **Mary Stith Shop.** In her will of 1813 she left this lot, its buildings, and much of her estate to her "coloured people" in gratitude for past services. Today the building functions as a music teacher's shop where students and teachers perform eighteenth-century music on colonial-era instruments.

Next door the thunderous ringing of hammers on hot metal and the smoke from the fires in seven forges announced that James Anderson and his blacksmiths were hard at work. During the Revolution Anderson made and repaired weapons for the American forces. He rented his shop, work force, and tools to the government.

James Anderson built the house around 1770. Today the **James Anderson House** contains an exhibit about archaeological discoveries. Audiovisual presentations explain how foundations and artifacts gave clues for reconstructing and refurnishing the Anderson House and forge.

A display of a typical bedroom includes authentic touches such as cracked tiles on the fireplace surround (things were seldom perfect in colonial days). Medicine bottles on the bedstand are a reminder that illness and pain were common in the eighteenth century and that medical treatment was rudimentary at best.

The seven forges operated by James Anderson in the eighteenth century have been rebuilt behind his house. The buildings housing the forges were reconstructed entirely by hand using only local

Brick House Tavern

James Anderson House
(Archaeological Exhibit)

materials and documented colonial construction methods and tools.

The first section of *James Anderson's Blacksmith Shop* contains a forge, tools, and a display that focuses on James Anderson and the demands placed on him as armorer of the colony during the Revolutionary War. As many as four forges operate simultaneously in the middle part. The types of blacksmithing that characterized James Anderson and his employees in the eighteenth century are demonstrated here. Smiths working at the two forges in the last section make nails that will be used in future construction projects (seasonal).

Next door, the **Brick House Tavern** was built as a rental property in the early 1760s. The building provided twelve residences with twelve separate entrances (six in front, six in the rear). Itinerant tradesmen and others with services or goods to sell would arrange for lodging here, advertise in the *Virginia Gazette,* and show their wares to customers in their rooms. If business seemed promising, they might settle down elsewhere in town; if not, they would move on. Over time, a surgeon, jeweler, watch repairer, milliner, wigmaker, and several tavern keepers, to name a few, called the Brick House Tavern home.

James Anderson House and Blacksmith Shop

The James Anderson House introduces visitors to the role of archaeology in Williamsburg. Part of a colonial bedroom has been reconstructed from precedents provided by excavated artifacts. Other exhibits show how the ground preserves them and the archaeologists retrieve them. One gallery presents many of the most complete pottery, glassware, and other artifacts, and another tells the history of James Anderson's home and his blacksmithing activities in the yard behind it.

Seven reconstructed forges in James Anderson's Blacksmith Shop behind the house operate much as they did in the eighteenth century. Several smithing operations are demonstrated.

Anderson's Blacksmith Shop 🛈

Mary Stith Shop 🛈
(Music Teacher's Room)

Orlando Jones Office and House

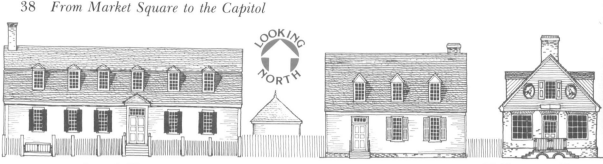

Prentis House   *Russell House*   **T** *Margaret Hunter*
                                                          ＊ *Shop (Milliner)*

From Botetourt Street to the Capitol

Tarpley's Store, a commercial establishment, is located on the south side of the street. Merchant James Tarpley erected and operated his store on this lot after it was subdivided in 1759. Newspaper advertisements show that local residents considered this block "the most public part of the city" and "the most convenient spot in this city for trade." Later in the century Alexander Purdie published a rival *Virginia Gazette* here. Purdie's newspaper bore the motto "Always for Liberty, and the Publick Good." He was appointed public printer just before the Revolution.

Merchandise typical of that sold in the eighteenth century is available at Tarpley's Store.

Across the street two residences, the **Prentis House** and the **Russell House,** break up the otherwise commercial character of the block. Behind the Prentis House is a charming garden open to visitors.

The **Margaret Hunter Shop** occupies a favorable spot on this busy "downtown" end of Duke of Gloucester Street. A 1774 advertisement gives a good idea of the

Margaret Hunter Shop
(*Milliner*)

An outstanding collection of American and English costume accessories is displayed in this original building. Milady of the twentieth century may step into a shop where the shelves are filled with eighteenth-century goods—hats, muffs, fans, gloves, jewelry, purses, shoes, and pieces of exquisite embroidery. Gentlemen will be pleased to find goods of interest to them as well.

The word "milliner" is derived from "Milaner," meaning a person who came from, or imported goods from, Milan, Italy. Thus a milliner in colonial days was an importer as well as a designer of fashionable clothes.

Tarpley's Store

The Golden Ball
(*Jeweler and* T
Engraver)

Unicorn's Horn and
John Carter's Store

The Golden Ball
(*Silversmith*)

Twentieth-century silversmiths create beautiful objects by hand in the eighteenth-century manner at the Golden Ball. Among the articles produced by the smiths are mote spoons, small teaspoons whose bowls are pierced with a decorative design. Mote spoons are useful for straining tea. Cabinets in the shop display mourning rings, paste buckles for shoes, pieces of English silver, and hollow ware based on English designs. A clock with a movement made and signed by James Craig, who lived and worked on this property from 1765 until the 1790s, is on display. The casting and forging of silver are practiced here.

Handmade silver hollow ware and gold and silver jewelry are offered for sale in the east side of the Golden Ball (ticket not required).

sorts of merchandise that Margaret Hunter stocked: "Jet necklaces and earrings, black love ribands, Sleeve Knots, Stuff Shoes for Ladies, Women's and children's riding habits, dressed and undressed Babies, toys, scotch snuff, and Busts of the late Lord Botetourt," a popular governor. Like some other shopkeepers in Williamsburg, Margaret Hunter lived above her store.

The **Margaret Hunter Shop,** an original structure, typically presents its gable end to the street. The sales area is in front, and there is a small counting room in the back. The brickwork is original except for a few patches. The blue green glaze on some of the bricks resulted from their having been nearest to the heat while they were being fired in the kiln.

The Golden Ball was the address of James Craig, a jeweler and silversmith from London, who established his business at this location in 1765. Craig once made a pair of earrings for Patsy Custis, the stepdaughter of George Washington. In 1772 Craig added a watchmaker to his staff and began advertising his store as the "Golden Ball," a trademark commonly used by jewelers and goldsmiths. Craig lived and worked on these premises with his family of five and one slave until he died in the early 1790s.

The original building on this site was built in 1724 and survived until 1907. A photograph, archaeological excavations of the foundations, and the recollections of former residents guided the reconstruction.

Next door, the double brick structure divided into the **Unicorn's Horn** and **John Carter's Store** was built in 1765 by two brothers. Dr. James Carter used the west portion as an apothecary shop under the distinctive sign of the unicorn's horn. His brother John ran a general store in the eastern half of the building.

Across the street is ***Wetherburn's Tavern,*** one of the most important of the town's surviving buildings because it has been so thoroughly documented—architecturally as a carefully studied original building, archaeologically through extensive excavations, and historically by surviving deeds, accounts, and a room-by-room inventory taken after the death of Henry Wetherburn, its long-time owner-operator, in 1760.

A colonial tavern was quite different from its modern namesake. In addition to serving liquor, it also offered lodging for travelers, meals, and a place for socializing and entertaining. Cards, dice, and conversation were as important as food and drink. Wetherburn's "great room," which measures twenty-five feet by twenty-five and occupies most of the west end of the first floor, occasionally served as an informal town hall in which scientific lectures, political gatherings, and balls were held.

A large-scale enterprise, Wetherburn's depended on slaves to cook, serve, clean, tend the garden, and groom customers' horses. Henry Wetherburn owned twelve slaves, among them eight women and two

Wetherburn's Tavern

A popular hostelry in eighteenth-century Williamsburg, Wetherburn's Tavern has been furnished with the aid of an inventory of the estate of Henry Wetherburn, tavern keeper from 1743 to 1760. Archaeological excavations on the site from 1964 to 1966 turned up more than two hundred thousand fragments of pottery, glass, and metal objects. Ceramics on display in the tavern match fragments of those excavated on the site. The outbuildings behind Wetherburn's form a domestic production area essential to the operation of a busy colonial tavern. The interpretation brings its day-by-day world to life.

* ***Charlton House***   * ***Wetherburn's Tavern***

Meet . . .
Caesar and Sarah

Caesar managed the stable and cared for horses of customers at Wetherburn's Tavern. He drove the tavern wagon around town and to nearby plantations like Carter's Grove where Wetherburn bought produce. Caesar always carried a travel permit from Wetherburn if he went as far away as Norfolk or Richmond because an unaccompanied black might be stopped and questioned.

Wetherburn's most valuable slave, Caesar had been appraised at seventy pounds in the inventory taken after his master's death in 1760. Wetherburn's widow, Anne, then took over the business. She depended heavily on slave labor to do much of the work at a busy tavern like Wetherburn's.

Sarah, Caesar's wife, managed the dairy. She milked the cows, separated and skimmed the milk, and churned butter. Sarah was valued at forty-five pounds.

Caesar and Sarah worshipped at Bruton Parish Church. Slaves sat apart in the north gallery. After divine services blacks could talk with one another and pass along the latest news and gossip.

Caesar and Sarah's two sons, William and Pompey, were both baptized in Bruton Church, William in 1762 and Pompey in 1764. The widow Wetherburn may have insisted that the boys be baptized, or perhaps it was done at Sarah's request. Records show that more than one thousand slaves were baptized in the church after mid-century.

young boys, Tom and Gabriel, who waited on tables. They would have lived in the attics over the kitchen and stable.

After Wetherburn's death in 1760, a long and detailed inventory of his estate listed the contents of the building room by room. It has been a principal guide in refurnishing the restored tavern. Additional information came from the painstaking excavations made by Colonial Williamsburg archaeologists, who recovered more than two hundred thousand artifacts from the site.

The outbuildings and the vegetable garden and yard form one of the most thoroughly researched dependency areas in Williamsburg. The dairy survives with its original framing. The other outbuildings, including the kitchen in which there is a huge fireplace, were reconstructed

on their eighteenth-century locations that were revealed by modern archaeological excavations.

Wigmaker Edward Charlton owned the neighboring ***Charlton House*** in 1770. Charlton kept an account book that details his wigmaking activities between 1769 and 1774. It shows that Charlton's customers included burgesses such as Thomas Jefferson, Patrick Henry, and Colonel Lewis Burwell of Kingsmill plantation and town residents—George Wythe, Thomas Everard, Peyton Randolph, and Peter Pelham to name a few—as well as local tavern keepers, merchants, and craftsmen. In addition to charges for wigs (brown dress bob wigs at two pounds, three shillings were popular), shaving, and hair dressing, Charlton also sold pairs of curls to the wives and daughters of his customers.

Williamsburg's working version of a wig shop, the **King's Arms Barber Shop** has been reconstructed. The barber pole, its red and white stripes signifying blood and bandages (harkening back to the days when barbers were also surgeons), is based on one in an eighteenth-century print by English artist William Hogarth.

Jane Vobe, one of Williamsburg's most successful tavern keepers, ran the **King's Arms Tavern.** In 1772 she announced her

King's Arms Barber Shop
(*Wigmaker*)

The wigmaker dresses hair and makes wigs in the eighteenth-century manner in this craft shop. In colonial days a wigmaker was also known as a perukemaker, a name derived from the French word "perruque," or "wig." An assortment of wigs and wigmaking tools and prints depicting wig styles and interiors of eighteenth century barber shops are on display.

location as "opposite the Raleigh, at the Sign of The King's Arms," a name that she changed to the Eagle Tavern after the Revolution.

The King's Arms, although outranked in historical fame by the Raleigh Tavern, has many associations with the past. During the Revolution, when Mrs. Vobe supplied food and drink to American troops, Baron von Steuben ran up a bill of nearly three hundred Spanish dollars for lodging, meals, and beverages.

The King's Arms offers traditional southern dishes served in an atmosphere reminiscent of colonial days.

The **John Coke Office** next door was named for an early nineteenth-century keeper of the Raleigh Tavern.

Across the street is the **Raleigh Tavern,** the foremost of Williamsburg's taverns in the eighteenth century. Established about 1717, the Raleigh grew in size and reputation through the years. Letters, diaries, newspaper advertisements, and other records indicate that the Raleigh was one of the most important taverns in colonial Virginia and, as such, served as a center for social, commercial, and political gatherings, small private and large public dinners, lectures and exhibits, and auctions of merchandise, property, and slaves.

During "Publick Times" when the courts were in session, the Raleigh was a center of social activity. Balls held in its Apollo Room were second in elegance only to those in the Governor's Palace. Planters and merchants gathered at its bar. Sturdy tavern tables were scarred by dice boxes; tobacco smoke from long clay pipes filled

John Coke Office

King's Arms Tavern

T *King's Arms Barber Shop (Wigmaker)*

Raleigh Tavern T

↑ *To Raleigh Tavern Kitchen*

the air. Good fellowship was sealed by a toast of Madeira or by a pint of ale drunk from a pewter tankard.

Although he generally stayed elsewhere, George Washington often noted in his diary that he "dined at the Raleigh." After one evening of revelry in 1763, twenty-year-old Thomas Jefferson, then reading law under the learned George Wythe's supervision, complained in a letter to a friend: "Last night as merry as agreeable company and dancing with Belinda in the *Apollo* could make me, I never could have thought the succeeding Sun would have seen me so wretched."

Public receptions were common. In 1775 Peyton Randolph was entertained at the Raleigh when he returned from serving as the president of the first Continental Congress which met in Philadelphia. The following year, Virginia troops in Williamsburg gave a farewell dinner in honor of their esteemed commander, Patrick Henry. After the Treaty of Paris ending the Revolution was proclaimed in the city, the citizens of the new republic concluded their triumphal parade with a celebration at the Raleigh Tavern. General Lafayette was welcomed on his return to Williamsburg in 1824 by a banquet in the Apollo Room.

The Raleigh Tavern's location, its convenient meeting rooms, and (one suspects) its proprietors' sympathy for the colonists' cause made it a center of political activities in Williamsburg during the 1760s and 1770s. In 1769, when Governor Botetourt dissolved the General Assembly because of its protest against the British Revenue Act, many indignant burgesses recon-

T

Raleigh Tavern

Williamsburg's most famous tavern in the eighteenth century, the Raleigh was the center of social, political, and business activities. Public receptions and balls were common, and the Phi Beta Kappa Society was founded here. Land, slaves, and goods were sold at the Raleigh Tavern, and it ranked with the Printing Office as a postal and news center. Patriots met here to voice their opposition to the policies of the British crown; important meetings at the Raleigh foreshadowed American independence.

vened at the tavern to draw up a boycott of British goods. Five years later, the Assembly again being dissolved, other nonimportation measures were agreed upon at the Raleigh after the shocking news reached Virginia that Great Britain had ordered the port of Boston closed. The "representatives of the people" also issued the call for delegates from all the colonies to meet in the first Continental Congress.

* *Alexander Craig House*   *Scrivener Store*

The Raleigh Tavern burned in 1859. Architects who reconstructed the building were aided by two drawings made in 1848, by insurance policies, and by archaeological excavations that revealed most of the original foundations of the tavern and many colonial artifacts. Inventories of the possessions of its eighteenth-century proprietors guided the refurnishing of the Raleigh. After the death of Anthony Hay in 1770, for example, the inventory listed most articles in the tavern.

The gentlemen of colonial Virginia and their ladies would find little changed if they returned to dance their minuets again. Charter members of the Phi Beta Kappa Society, founded in Williamsburg in 1776, could once more meet in the Apollo Room. The Raleigh's pervasive spirit of hospitality is well expressed in the motto gilded over the Apollo Room mantel: *Hilaritas Sapientiae et Bonae Vitae Proles*— "Jollity, the offspring of wisdom and good living."

In the eighteenth century the Raleigh Tavern backyard would have included a kitchen garden, a chicken coop, and a laundry area. Its stables, paddock, and a large agricultural tract—about twenty acres in all—were located two blocks north of the tavern.

Today visitors can purchase bread, cookies, and other baked products at the Raleigh Tavern Bake Shop in the Raleigh Tavern Kitchen (ticket not required).

Commercial establishments lined nearly all the rest of Duke of Gloucester Street from the Raleigh to the Capitol. The ***Alexander Craig House, Scrivener Store,*** and ***Nicolson Store*** were, respectively, a saddle and harness shop, grocery, and general store. A proliferation of taverns occupied this end of the street. The ***John Crump House, Burdett's Ordinary,*** and ***Shields' Tavern*** competed for the trade of the traveling public. A Russian traveler to Wil-

The Apollo Room.

Pasteur & Galt Apothecary Shop 🔳   * *Nicolson Store*   *John Crump House*   *Burdett's Ordinary*

liamsburg in 1779 depicted the John Crump House in a sketch now preserved in Leningrad.

In the ***Pasteur & Galt Apothecary Shop,*** drug jars of blue and white delft hold the latest in medical remedies. There are cinchona pills for malaria, tincture of benzoin for wounds, and a new drug used by colonial doctors, foxglove. Each contains active ingredients still used in modern medicine. There are splints, a fracture box, and books with the latest in eighteenth-century medical theory, including how to inoculate for smallpox.

During the years of Dr. John Galt's practice in Williamsburg, 1769–1808, the shop also sold tobacco for a gentleman's pipe, as well as vermicelli, anchovies, spermaceti, ether, and patent medicines.

Dr. Galt's diplomas in surgery, anatomy, general medicine, and midwifery, all earned from London hospitals, hang in the Apothecary Shop today. Eighteenth-century pharmacopoeias and surgical tools used for amputations, removal of bladder stones, and other common procedures are also on display.

🔳

Pasteur & Galt Apothecary Shop

On display today is an imposing array of elixirs, ointments, and surgical instruments used by colonial apothecaries, most of whom were also doctors. An herb garden behind the shop is open to the public.

Shields' Tavern

Meet . . .
William Byrd II

William Byrd II (1674–1744) was the master of West-over plantation, a large estate on the James River about a five-hour horseback ride from Williamsburg. Educated in England where he was trained in the law, Byrd had a taste for classical literature and a knowledge of the world of fashion. He cultivated a group of distinguished friends. When he returned to Virginia in 1705, William Byrd II was deemed the colony's most polished gentleman.

A career of public service was the natural inheritance of a young man of Byrd's position. He soon received an appointment to the powerful Council, and for the rest of his life he served as an influential member of that body. He also represented the colony of Virginia as official agent in London and proved to be a capable diplomat.

Byrd was a tireless and accurate observer of Virginia life. For over thirty years he recorded his daily activities in a series of diaries written in a secret shorthand cipher.

Byrd often came to Williamsburg to fulfill his public duties. On October 15, 1709, he noted: "I rose at 3 o'clock . . . and proceeded to Williamsburg by moonshine." Gay and fun loving, Byrd did not devote all of his time in the capital to business. On one occasion he went to visit the governor and they "drank a bottle of claret and were merry till 10 o'clock." Byrd often patronized Shields', Wetherburn's, or one of the other local taverns: "We played at cards and I won about £4. It was one o'clock before I got to bed."

Nearest the Capitol on Duke of Gloucester Street are the Palmer House, on the south side, and the Dora Armistead House, on the north.

Lawyer and bursar of the College of William and Mary, John Palmer built the ***Palmer House*** at mid-century on the site of an old store. During the Civil War, it served as the military headquarters, first for Confederate General Joseph Johnston and then for General George McClellan, the commander of the Union forces.

The ***Dora Armistead House,*** the Victorian structure across the street, reminds today's visitors that the town lived on after 1780, although much changed from its colonial character. Within recent memory, a discreet sign, "Guests," hung from the porch, and many twentieth-century visitors thus lodged on the street where their forebears had hired rooms two hundred years earlier. This privately owned structure, which has been restored to its early twentieth-century appearance, is exhibited by the Association for the Preservation of Virginia Antiquities.

* ***Dora Armistead House***

Merchants met in the open area that terminates Duke of Gloucester Street, just before the Capitol wall, to set the prices of tobacco and other agricultural products and to trade in commercial paper. Called the ***Exchange,*** it functioned much like a modern commodities market, dealing in futures and risk. After the capital moved to Richmond in 1780, however, it like Williamsburg as a whole–decreased in importance.

A stroll down Duke of Gloucester Street from Market Square to the Capitol takes visitors through a busy section of Williamsburg. Prentis and Tarpley's stores offer the wide range of merchandise stocked by eighteenth-century general stores, while the shops of the milliner, silversmith, barber, and apothecary represent some of the specialized goods and services available to colonial consumers. Wetherburn's and the Raleigh recall the hustle and bustle of tavern life as travelers and townsfolk alike came to find a warming drink, a bite to eat, or a bed for the night. The Printing Office is a reminder of the importance of communications in the eighteenth century. Finally, the blacksmithing operations at the James Anderson site re-create the light industry that developed shortly before the American Revolution.

* ***Palmer House***

The Senior Corps of the Colonial Williamsburg Fifes and Drums steps out proudly.

Shopping Opportunities

PRENTIS STORE
(ticket not required)

Goods representative of those sold in eighteenth-century stores are sold here: pottery, baskets, blankets, candles, soap, tobacco and pipes, cooper's items, and tools.

POST OFFICE
(ticket not required)

Books, prints, maps, stationery, seals and sealing wax, newspapers, games, and playing cards—items typical of those sold at the colonial post office—are available.

HUNTER'S STORE *(ticket not required)*

The grocer's shop offers food products such as Virginia ham, jams and jellies, cider, tea, and coffee.

TARPLEY'S STORE
(ticket not required)

Tarpley's Store features merchandise typical of that sold in the eighteenth century. Toys, tricorn and straw hats, wooden boxes, candies, dried fruits, horn products, soap, and jewelry are some of the many items available here.

RALEIGH TAVERN BAKE SHOP *(ticket not required)*

Delicious breads and other baked goods—gingerbread, cookies, and tarts—are featured at the Raleigh Tavern Bake Shop.

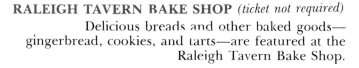

THE GOLDEN BALL
(ticket not required)

For sale are items of hand-made silver hollow ware and gold and silver jewelry.

American Express, Mastercard, and Visa credit cards are accepted at Colonial Williamsburg retail outlets.

Dining Opportunities

KING'S ARMS TAVERN (ticket not required)

Considered one of the most "genteel" eighteenth-century taverns, the King's Arms was patronized by a select clientele that included George Washington and General Thomas Nelson, Jr., of Yorktown, a revolutionary leader who became Virginia's fourth governor.

Traditional southern dishes—peanut soup, Virginia ham, fried chicken, game pie, and Sally Lunn bread—are featured at the King's Arms. Seasonal light meals are served in the grape arbor.

American Express, Mastercard, and Visa credit cards are accepted.

The King's Arms Tavern specializes in traditional southern dishes served in the hospitable atmosphere of long ago.

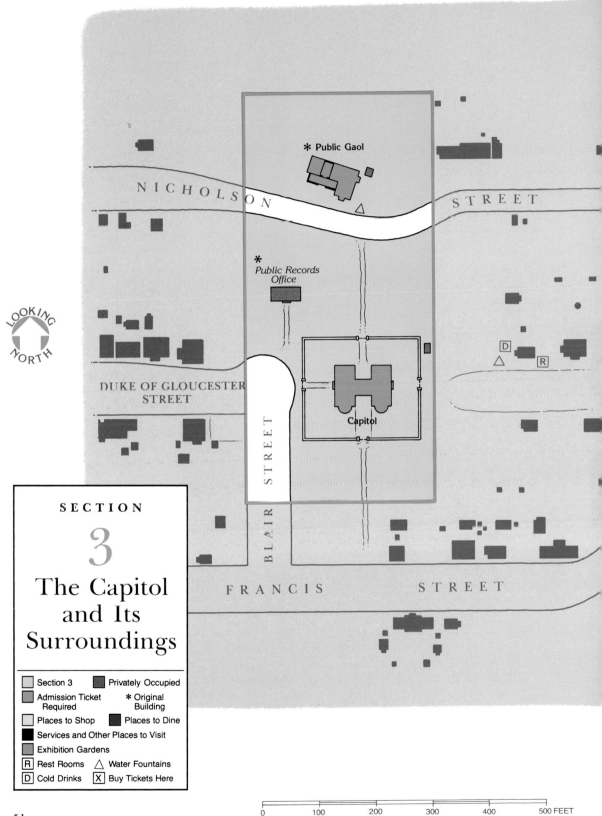

LOOKING NORTH

* Public Gaol

* Public Records Office

Capitol

NICHOLSON STREET

DUKE OF GLOUCESTER STREET

BLAIR STREET

FRANCIS STREET

D
R

SECTION

3

The Capitol
and Its
Surroundings

Section 3		Privately Occupied
Admission Ticket Required		* Original Building
Places to Shop		Places to Dine
Services and Other Places to Visit		
Exhibition Gardens		
R Rest Rooms		△ Water Fountains
D Cold Drinks		X Buy Tickets Here

0   100   200   300   400   500 FEET

Capitol T

The Capitol and Its Surroundings

FOR eighty years Williamsburg was the political center of Virginia, one of England's largest, wealthiest, and most populous colonies. Here laws and justice were made and administered on behalf of all eighteenth-century Virginians. The first and second Capitol buildings, the Public Gaol, and the Public Records Office were visible reminders that these buildings and the activities that went on inside them gave Williamsburg a political importance second to that of no other colonial capital.

At the Capitol, the General Assembly debated and framed legislation and the courts dispensed justice. Most of the important records of the colony—legal documents of every kind—were kept in the Public Records Office. Nearby, at the Public Gaol, Virginians accused of felonies or imprisoned for debts languished until their cases could be heard in court.

Spring and fall sessions of the General Court, less regular summer and winter sessions of the criminal court, and sessions of the General Assembly, which were convened by the governor, provided the formal occasions that brought the Capitol area to life. Other, more informal activities animated the scene year-round because the bureaucratic machinery that kept the wheels of government turning operated continuously.

The H-shaped plan of the ***Capitol*** is an early example of an architectural design successfully devised for a specific purpose. It also reflects the makeup of Virginia's colonial government.

Representative government in Virginia

began in 1619. As the General Assembly evolved, it was composed of the Council and the House of Burgesses, each of which met separately.

The east wing of the Capitol contained the Hall of the House of Burgesses on the first floor and committee rooms for the burgesses on the second. The House of Burgesses, the lower house of the legislature, consisted of two members elected by the landowners of each county and one member each from Jamestown, Williamsburg, Norfolk, and the College of William and Mary.

The west wing housed the General Courtroom on the first floor and the Council Chamber on the second. The Council, made up of twelve leading colonists appointed for life by the king, constituted the upper house of the legislature. They also assisted the governor by acting as a council of state. In its legislative capacity, the Council met in the elegantly furnished Council Chamber. Each wing had its own staircase.

The General Assembly convened periodically in the Capitol to act on a wide range of legislation. In the course of a session, which could have lasted a few days or several weeks, the upper and lower houses might have considered the petition of a veteran for public assistance or frontier settlers seeking the formulation of a new county. They could divide large counties into smaller ones or move a county's courthouse to a more central location. They considered aiding other colonies in wartime, while at the same time establishing Virginia's own frontier defenses. They settled public claims and levied taxes to pay for them. And, as the imperial crisis of the 1760s and 1770s worsened, they spent more and more time debating remonstrations to submit to King George III and Parliament.

If the two houses deadlocked in trying to pass a bill already accepted by one or the other, representatives from the Council and the burgesses met jointly in the second floor chamber located over the entrance portico. In effect this conference room formed a bridge between the two buildings. The architecture of the Capitol thus aided the process of mediation between the two houses. Morning prayers were also held in the conference room.

The foundations of the original building were laid in 1701. Impatient with meeting at the College, Virginia's lawmakers moved into the new Capitol in 1704, a year before its completion.

As a drastic precaution against fire, Wil-

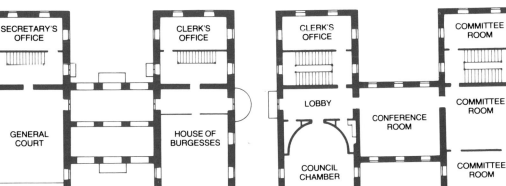

Plan of the ground floor of the reconstructed Capitol.

Plan of the upper floor of the reconstructed Capitol.

Capitol

The House of Burgesses and the Council, the two houses of the legislature in colonial Virginia, met at the Capitol. Patrick Henry's fiery 1765 "Caesar-Brutus" speech, the May 15, 1776, Resolution for Independence, which led directly to the July 4 Declaration in Philadelphia, and the introduction of Thomas Jefferson's Statute for Religious Freedom occurred on this site.

The General Court, the colony's highest judicial tribunal, met twice yearly in the Capitol, which has been rebuilt on its original foundations.

William Gooch, a second Capitol, completed in 1753, was built. It incorporated the surviving walls of its predecessor but differed in appearance. After the removal of Virginia's government to Richmond in 1780, the second building fell into disrepair, and in 1832 it too was destroyed by fire.

Before reconstruction could be undertaken, Colonial Williamsburg faced a dilemma: should the first or second building rise again on the old foundations? The second Capitol was of greater historic interest since it witnessed the events of the years before the Revolution, but the first Capitol could lay claim to greater architectural distinction, its rounded ends, for instance, being unique. Moreover, long searching of the architectural evidence disclosed voluminous information about the earlier building, whereas few records were available for the later one. As a result, the first Capitol was reconstructed.

Two courts met regularly in the Capitol. The General Court, the highest court of the colony, convened in April and October to hear both civil and criminal cases. The governor and the twelve members of the Council served as the justices of the General Court. After 1710 the Court of Oyer

The Great Union flag (left) became the national standard of Great Britain and her colonies in 1707. It flies today over the Capitol. On May 15, 1776, the Grand Union flag (right) became the first American flag to fly in Williamsburg.

liamsburg's first Capitol was designed without chimneys, and the use of fire, candles, or tobacco was strictly prohibited. In time such safeguards were sacrificed to necessity and convenience. A secretary complained, for example, that his records were "exposed by the Damps." Two chimneys were therefore added in 1723. Despite precautions, however, the building was gutted by fire on January 30, 1747, "and the naked Brick Walls only left standing."

With the encouragement of Governor

and Terminer (meaning "to hear and decide"), presided over by the councillors alone, heard criminal cases at sessions in June and December.

Punishment for serious crimes was harsh in the eighteenth century, and the death penalty was sometimes invoked for offenses such as arson, horse stealing, forg-

The Prelude to Independence

On May 6, 1776, delegates to Virginia's Fifth Convention met at the Capitol in Williamsburg. Realizing the importance of the tasks that lay ahead, the voters had elected an able group of experienced legislators to represent them, including Patrick Henry, Edmund Pendleton, Robert Carter Nicholas, George Mason, Edmund Randolph, and James Madison. The Convention was in close touch with the Virginia delegation to the Second Continental Congress meeting in Philadelphia. Virginia's representatives included George Wythe, Thomas Jefferson, Benjamin Harrison, Thomas Nelson, Carter Braxton, and the Lee brothers, Richard Henry and Francis Lightfoot.

For more than a year the thirteen colonies had been resisting British authority. For almost two years Virginians had been governing themselves in defiance of British authority. Virginia's revolution began in Williamsburg on May 26, 1774, when the House of Burgesses, although dissolved by Governor Lord Dunmore, met at the Raleigh Tavern to form a Virginia Association. The burgesses called for a convention of Virginia delegates to meet in Williamsburg on August 1. The First Virginia Convention set up committees of safety in every county and encouraged the other colonies to meet at Philadelphia in the First Continental Congress. There, under the presidency of Peyton Randolph, Virginians took the lead in seeking the redress of American grievances and a union of all the colonies to accomplish that end.

Early in 1776, sparked by Tom Paine's *Common Sense,* by the embattled farmers of New England, and by the people and leaders of Virginia, the call for independence spread like wildfire through the American colonies. Now, meeting in convention in Williamsburg on May 15, Virginia's patriot leaders deliberately created a new, free commonwealth and called upon Congress in Philadelphia to declare the independence of the American people from the tyranny of King George III. Acting on the resolution of the Virginia Convention, Richard Henry Lee presented a motion for independence in the Continental Congress on June 7, 1776. A committee of five headed by Thomas Jefferson prepared the draft declaration. Congress voted to approve the motion for independence on July 2 and adopted the declaration without dissent on July 4.

At Williamsburg the period from early May to late July 1776 is commemorated as "The Prelude to Independence." It honors the time when the founding fathers of Virginia asked Congress to declare the colonies independent and established a new form of government for the Commonwealth of Virginia. On July 25, 1776, Benjamin Waller read the Declaration of Independence to a huge throng gathered at the Courthouse. Illuminations and the firing of cannon marked the crowd's approval. Williamsburg, and most often the Capitol, had been the scene of many of the events leading to American independence.

ery, burglary—and piracy. Clemency might be granted, however, to first offenders or criminals with particularly moving pleas. In 1727 convicted teenage pirate John Vidal, who pitifully protested that he "never intended to go a-pirating" and "with a weeping heart" begged for mercy, was granted his majesty's most gracious pardon.

Ceremony and formality characterized the proceedings of these legislative and judicial bodies and the behavior of their members. When a new governor arrived, he was customarily met by a delegation and conveyed directly to the Capitol to be sworn to the king's commission. The opening ceremony of the General Assembly was patterned after the opening of Parliament. Governor Botetourt rode down Duke of Gloucester Street to the Capitol for the

Patrick Henry, the first governor of the Commonwealth of Virginia.

opening of the General Assembly in a gilded state coach drawn by six matching gray horses.

Burgesses assembled in the Council Chamber, took their oaths of office in the presence of the Council, and returned to the House to elect a speaker. Upon the governor's formal approval of the speaker's election, the mace of the House, which had been placed under the table, was returned to the table top and the burgesses proceeded with their legislative business.

Parliamentary privilege exercised by the English Parliament extended to the House of Burgesses to protect the House and its members against slander. In 1723 burgess Mathew Kemp complained that attorney William Hopkins had uttered "several rude Contemptious and undecent Expressions" about Kemp's conduct in the House. The burgesses found Hopkins guilty of contempt and ordered him to kneel, "acknowledge his Offence, and ask pardon of this House and Mr. Kemp." Hopkins refused. The burgesses next ordered that Hopkins, wearing a sign that proclaimed his offenses, be led from the Capitol to the College and back again. Then he was to be imprisoned. Upon hearing this, a chastened Hopkins knelt, expressed sorrow, and prayed mercy of the House, which fined and then discharged him.

The speaker's chair in the House of Burgesses was probably made by a Williamsburg cabinetmaker for the first Capitol about 1730. It moved to Richmond with the rest of the state's possessions in 1780. It was returned to the Capitol in Williamsburg through the courtesy of the General Assembly of Virginia.

Some of the colony's most powerful officials had offices in the Capitol. The secretary, usually a member of the Council, was appointed by the king. His office issued all land patents and most other documents, including naturalization papers and passports, that required the seal of the colony.

The auditor examined all colonial revenue accounts and forwarded them to Treasury officials in London, while the receiver general took in and disbursed the colony's "royal revenues." The attorney general also had an office in the Capitol. He gave legal advice to the governor and his Council, prosecuted criminal cases before the General Court, and, after 1720, served as the sole judge of the Vice Admiralty Court. Because of his role as the king's attorney, the attorney general was never a councillor.

A memorable historical event occurred at the Capitol on May 15, 1776, when Virginia's legislators pledged their lives and fortunes by taking the daring step of declaring their full freedom from England. The burgesses adopted a resolution for American independence without a dissenting vote.

On June 7, 1776, Richard Henry Lee, one of Virginia's delegates, acting on this resolution, introduced a motion for independence on the floor of the Continental Congress at Philadelphia. This led directly to the Declaration of Independence, drafted largely by Thomas Jefferson, who had stood at the half-open door of the House of Burgesses in Williamsburg eleven years before to hear Patrick Henry thunder his defiance of Parliament and king.

Before a separate records office was

Virginia's Famous Signers

". . . we mutually pledge to each other our Lives, our Fortunes, and our sacred Honor."

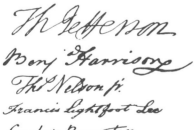

In the crucial decade before the American Revolution, Williamsburg was a training ground for a remarkable body of men. When it became clear that war with Great Britain could not be avoided, George Wythe, Richard Henry Lee, Thomas Jefferson, Benjamin Harrison, Thomas Nelson, Francis Lightfoot Lee, and Carter Braxton met in Philadelphia with representatives from the other colonies to declare independence from the mother country. On July 4, 1776, the Continental Congress formally adopted the Declaration of Independence and took the first momentous step toward establishing a new nation.

George Washington did not sign the Declaration of Independence because in July 1776 he was in New York preparing to defend Manhattan against the British.

* *Public Records Office*

built, the most important public papers of the colony were stored in the secretary's office next to the General Courtroom. The chief clerk of the secretary's office and his deputy oversaw a vast domain of records in the form of bound volumes and of endless files of loose papers tied up in the red tape that had been used by bureaucrats to secure legal and official documents since the seventeenth century. Here generations of clerk-apprentices scribbled away, learning their trade.

When the Capitol burned in 1747, officials fortunately were able to save a number of records that included land office records, executive papers of the clerk of the Council, and the files of the clerk of the House of Burgesses. Afterward it took nearly a year to sort them all out.

After the fire the burgesses and Council agreed in principle on the necessity of building a **Public Records Office.** But while the burgesses' approval was delayed by a debate about whether to move the capital farther inland, the Council acted decisively. It contracted for and oversaw the erection of a repository for the public records. The building was completed by December 1748 at a cost of £367 19s. 6d., paid for out of the royal revenues.

The building was clearly designed to avoid fire at all costs. There was neither basement nor attic, the original floor was paved with stones, and the interior walls and window jambs were plastered-over brick. Little wood was used in the building. There were, however, four fireplaces in the three-room structure to provide heat in winter and drive off the damp and mold in summer. Tidewater humidity can be as destructive as fire to paper and leather.

It would be hard to overestimate the potential influence in the colony of the office of the secretary. Perhaps the most significant of his privileges was the power to appoint the clerks of all the courts in Virginia. To supply a trained cadre of these young men, five to seven apprentice clerks were always at work in the secretary's office. Sent there at their family's expense to serve an apprenticeship of seven years, they then waited their turn to be named to the next vacant clerkship. This system was successful in producing a body of clerks who had been trained to the same standards.

After the capital and its records moved to Richmond in 1780, the Public Records Office was occupied for a time by the Court of Admiralty under Justice Benjamin Waller. When the Capitol became a private grammar school, the Public Records Office was refitted as a home for the headmaster.

The **Public Gaol,** just north of the Capitol on Nicholson Street, affords today grim evidence of crime and punishment in colonial America.

Accused offenders were imprisoned in the Gaol only until their cases came to trial

Meet . . . Adam Craig

Born in Williamsburg in 1759, Adam Craig was the son of James Craig, the jeweler who owned the Golden Ball. Adam grew up during the eventful years preceding the American Revolution. For Adam it was an exciting time and a time of high hopes.

Adam normally would have been expected either to follow in his father's footsteps or to learn some other craft, but he had good reason to believe that he would not become an artisan like his father. In the early 1770s James Craig secured an apprenticeship in the secretary's office for his son. Adam knew that by long custom the colonial secretary filled vacant county clerkships with senior apprentices from his office. Adam also knew that the position of county clerk was both a lucrative and a socially prominent post. For the son of a craftsman to attain such an appointment would fulfill his and his father's dreams of social advancement.

At the Public Records Office Adam entered into a seven-year course of training under the tutelage of chief clerk Benjamin Waller. He developed a legible hand, learned the proper forms for all legal documents, and gained an understanding of the legal system. Adam proved to be an eager and capable student.

In 1776, when he was only seventeen, Adam's plans for the future suffered a severe setback. The new state constitution ended the right of the secretary to appoint county clerks. Left with no sure employment, Adam and four fellow apprentices petitioned the state legislature to make them county clerks. The petition was clearly so self-serving that the five young men were told to withdraw it.

Despite an uncertain future, Adam continued his training. In the end, his skill and ability earned him the career he wanted. When he was only twenty-one Adam was appointed deputy clerk of Virginia's General Court and he moved to Richmond. Adam became chief clerk of the General Court, clerk of Henrico County, and clerk of the Hustings Court of the city of Richmond before his death in 1808.

---

in the Capitol before either the General Court or the Court of Oyer and Terminer, the criminal court. Insolvent debtors awaiting relief or mercy were occasionally held in the Gaol. Their numbers were greatly reduced by a 1772 act that made creditors wholly responsible for their debt-ors' maintenance and which tripled the fees charged for their board. Runaway slaves were detained until their masters claimed them and paid their expenses.

The Gaol served at times as a madhouse and as a military prison. Until the Public Hospital opened in 1773, some mentally ill

*   *Public Gaol* T

individuals were occasionally confined in the Gaol. In the early years of the Revolution the Gaol was crowded with captured British redcoats, tory sympathizers, and accused traitors, deserters, and spies.

Prison conditions in colonial days would be judged both crude and cruel by modern standards. The use of leg irons, handcuffs, and chains seems inhumane. Even if the night was bitterly cold, prisoners of every description bedded down with only a thin blanket. A diet of "salt beef damaged, and Indian meal" could not have been very appetizing. Yet prisoners were allowed to converse and walk about the exercise yard during the day, use the crude sanitary arrangements (the thrones in each cell), and were given "physick," or medicine, when ill. Prisoners with money or accommodating friends could purchase food and liquor from one of the taverns nearby or obtain clothing and blankets to supplement those issued at the Gaol.

Legislation that was passed in 1701 called for the construction of a "substantial Brick Prison" twenty by thirty feet. The act further provided for an adjoining walled exercise yard. Debtors' cells were added in 1711, while quarters for the gaoler were built in 1722. In its present form the Wil-

T

Public Gaol

Described in the eighteenth century as a "strong sweet Prison," the Public Gaol (pronounced "jail") is a grim reminder of crime and punishment in colonial Virginia. Common criminals awaiting their trials and debtors unable to settle their accounts were imprisoned here—as were pirates, marauding Indians, and runaway slaves.

During the American Revolution, Henry Hamilton, the British governor of the Northwest Territory, widely known as the "Hair Buyer" because he was believed to pay his Indian allies for American scalps, was detained in the Public Gaol at Williamsburg.

Meet . . . Peter Pelham

Peter Pelham, who served as the keeper of the Public Gaol from 1771 until 1779, was a man of many talents. Born in England in 1721, Pelham came to America in 1726 with his father and spent a number of years in Boston where he studied music and became the organist at Trinity Church.

Pelham moved to Williamsburg around 1750. He was the organist at Bruton Parish Church, taught young ladies to play the harpsichord and spinet, and served as musical director when *The Beggar's Opera* was first performed in the city.

Like many musicians then and now, Pelham's art and talent were insufficient to maintain his growing family. He and his wife, Ann, had fourteen children, some of whom died in infancy. He supplemented his income by acting as a clerk to Governors Fauquier and Botetourt. Governor Dunmore, Lord Botetourt's successor, named Pelham keeper of the Public Gaol.

After Pelham assumed his duties at the Gaol, he conveniently—and habitually—took a prisoner to the church to pump the organ while he played. It appears that Pelham was more successful as an organist than as a gaoler. He was criticized for occasionally "appearing much disguised with liquor," and some felt that his laxness led to a number of escapes. An inquiry ordered by the General Assembly cleared Pelham of all charges, however.

---

liamsburg Gaol has three rooms on the first floor—a large one for the gaoler and two smaller ones for male and female prisoners respectively—and "chambers" in the attic for the gaoler's use and the confinement of petty offenders.

The gaolkeepers, who often served as custodians of the Capitol, were appointed by the governor. Most of them did not live on the premises. Gaolers had a rough and dangerous job for which they were paid a modest salary. The first keeper, John Redwood, received thirty pounds annually, an amount supplemented by prisoners' fees and eventually increased by the General Assembly.

The Gaol served colony and commonwealth until 1780. A portion of the original building continued to be used by the city of Williamsburg as its jail until 1910. Part of the brickwork of the Gaol's massive walls is original. Shackles unearthed in the course of its restoration are evidence of the bleak life of a colonial criminal.

When the rebuilt Capitol was dedicated in 1934, Mr. John D. Rockefeller, Jr., addressed the House of Delegates and the Senate of the Commonwealth of Virginia, meeting in joint session: "What a temptation to sit in silence and let the past speak to us of those great patriots whose voices once resounded in these halls, and whose farseeing wisdom, high courage, and unselfish devotion to the common good will ever be an inspiration to noble living."

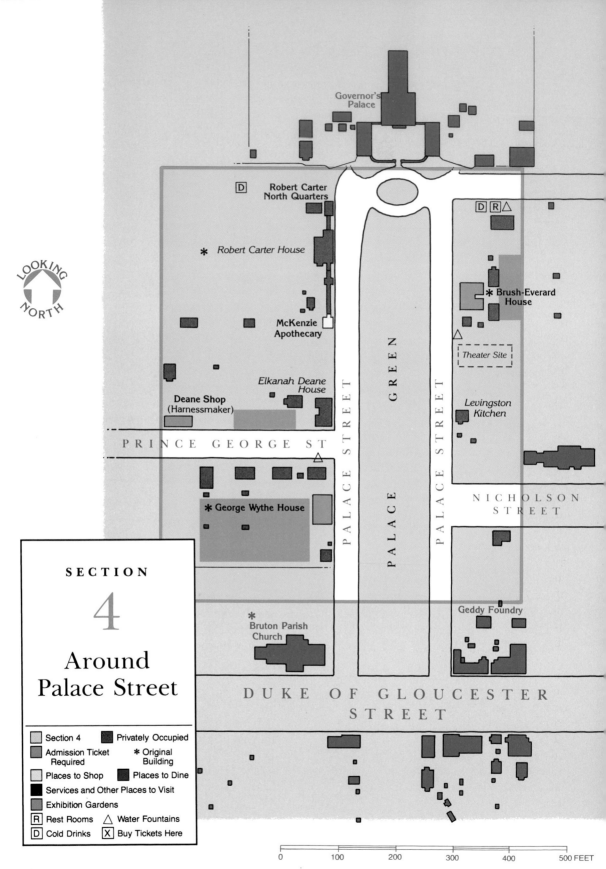

LOOKING NORTH

Governor's
Palace

D Robert Carter
North Quarters

D R △

* Robert Carter House

* Brush-Everard
House

McKenzie
Apothecary

△

P A L A C E   S T R E E T

G R E E N

P A L A C E

P A L A C E   S T R E E T

Theater Site

Levingston
Kitchen

Elkanah Deane
House

Deane Shop
(Harnessmaker)

P R I N C E   G E O R G E   S T

△

* George Wythe House

N I C H O L S O N
S T R E E T

Geddy Foundry

*
Bruton Parish
Church

D U K E   O F   G L O U C E S T E R
S T R E E T

SECTION

4

Around
Palace Street

▢ Section 4	▪ Privately Occupied
▪ Admission Ticket Required	∗ Original Building
▢ Places to Shop	▪ Places to Dine
▪ Services and Other Places to Visit	
▪ Exhibition Gardens	
R Rest Rooms	△ Water Fountains
D Cold Drinks	X Buy Tickets Here

0   100   200   300   400   500 FEET

Around Palace Street

WHEN eighteenth-century visitors turned north from Duke of Gloucester Street onto Palace Street, they looked down a long expanse of open ground that terminated at the Governor's Palace. One contemporary described the vista: "Toward the center of the city . . . is the Governor's Palace, very well built, very spacious, with a big lawn . . . which forms a pretty avenue." Rows of catalpa trees planted one hundred feet apart flanked the green.

The spacious homes built here after mid-century on large lots gave this part of Williamsburg a more residential air than the densely developed section of town near the Capitol. These well-built houses had a formal appearance that bespoke the education and civility that set their "gentle" owners apart from the "simple" artisan or tradesman. But such distinctions did not characterize Palace Street in the early years of the eighteenth century when more modest one and one-half story houses shared the green with a tavern, a theater, and several craftsmen's shops.

Even after mid-century, as wealthy Virginians began to reshape the style of their houses in keeping with newly acquired refined manners, Palace Street did not become completely residential. From the 1730s on, unsightly piles of coal used to fuel the Geddy forge and foundry were in full view in the backyard of the James Geddy House on the corner of Palace and Duke of Gloucester streets. In the 1760s a lead manufactory was in operation beyond the Wythe property; by the 1770s a busy coachworks was located behind the Elkanah Deane House. In the eighteenth century polite society had not yet chosen to remove itself completely from the presence of the workaday world, and mixed residential neighborhoods, such as that around Palace Street, were common.

Behind the houses on Palace Street, like elsewhere in Williamsburg, lived and worked the town's slaves. Signs of their presence—the currycombs of the grooms, the pots and pans of the cooks, and the pails of the housemaids—could be found all around these work areas. By the time of the Revolution fully half of the town's population was black.

Here and there, tucked into corners or hidden in lofts above kitchens, stables, and other outbuildings were their scant personal possessions: a straw-filled mattress, one or two extra pieces of clothing, an occasional fiddle or banjo. These few material goods only begin to suggest the full cultural life that Africans and their descendants created in the New World. In Williamsburg's backyards black men and women courted, married, and reared children. They told African folk tales adapted to life in Virginia, taught their children how to cope with the harsh realities of slavery, and attempted to subvert the system by harboring runaway slaves.

William Levingston bought three lots at the corner of Palace and Nicholson streets in 1716. Soon afterward he built a house, kitchen, and other outbuildings. He also constructed a playhouse and laid out a bowling green. Today, the reconstructed *Levingston Kitchen* is all that remains on the site.

* Brush-Everard House ⊤

Archaeologists have unearthed the foundations of Levingston's playhouse, which was the first theater in colonial America. It measured eighty-six and one-half feet long by thirty feet wide and stood at least two stories high, about the same size as English provincial theaters of the period. Wooden posts now mark each of the vanished building's four corners.

Levingston brought actors and dancers to Virginia as indentured servants, and he contracted with Charles and Mary Stagg, who were to act themselves and to train other performers. In 1718, to celebrate the birthday of King George I, Governor Spotswood sponsored the first play known to have been staged at the theater.

Although performances sometimes attracted a boisterous, rowdy audience, the gentry also frequented the playhouse. In the eighteenth century the theater was an important civilizing influence, educating people in socially acceptable ways to behave and edifying them with dramas of virtue tried and virtue triumphant.

Levingston briefly operated a tavern at his house next door. Theatergoers could drink, eat, bed down, or socialize around his bowling green. Impresario Levingston soon encountered financial difficulties and had to mortgage the property.

The building continued to be used periodically. In 1736 "the young Gentlemen of the College" performed *The Tragedy of Cato. The Busy-Body, The Recruiting Officer,* and *The Beaux' Stratagem* were also presented.

This location changed in appearance and character through the years. By the mid-1730s Dr. George Gilmer, a successful apothecary-surgeon, had acquired the property, moved into the house, and built an apothecary shop on the corner.

In 1745 Dr. Gilmer sold the theater to a group of subscribers who gave it to the city to be remodeled for a courthouse. The Hustings Court (Williamsburg's municipal court) met here until the city and James City County joined in erecting the brick Courthouse on Market Square in 1770. About the same time the old playhouse was demolished.

In 1788 St. George Tucker bought the house that Levingston had built. Tucker moved it to a more desirable location

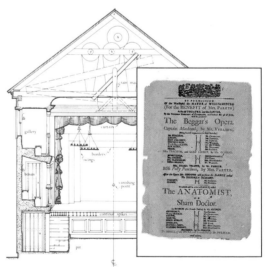

The drawing is a conjectural reconstruction of an eighteenth-century theater. The original playbill is for THE BEGGAR'S OPERA, *which was first performed in Williamsburg in 1768. Peter Pelham, organist at Bruton Parish Church and keeper of the Public Gaol, supervised the musical part of the production.*

Theater Site   *Levingston Kitchen*

fronting on Market Square, which had, since the 1750s, become an increasingly important focus of town life.

John Brush, gunsmith, armorer, and first keeper of the Magazine on Market

Brush-Everard House

The Brush-Everard House was owned by Thomas Everard, a wealthy civic leader, from about 1755 until 1781. Everard enlarged the house and embellished the interior with woodwork that is noteworthy for its remarkable carving. It may have been done by the joiner who worked on the magnificent staircase that is the pride of Carter's Grove plantation.

A library assembled in the Brush-Everard House was based on a list of books compiled by Thomas Jefferson for a well-to-do planter of average intellectual interests. Works on law, philosophy, religion, history, science, drama, and the classics are included among the three hundred volumes.

Square, built the **Brush-Everard House** on this property in 1717. After Brush died in 1727, it had several different owners.

Dancing master and painter William Dering bought the house in 1742. Although he was not a member of the gentry himself, Dering associated with the upper classes. By the mid-eighteenth century planters turned to dancing masters because they wanted to learn the elaborate manners that an increasingly fashion conscious society valued. The ability to dance a minuet and to dance it well in the Governor's Palace or the Apollo Room at the Raleigh Tavern meant that a person was a cultured member of polite society.

Thomas Everard acquired the property about 1755 and lived there for twenty-five years. A wealthy and respected local leader, Everard was active in civic affairs. He twice served as mayor of Williamsburg—in 1766 and 1771—and he was on the vestry of Bruton Parish Church. Everard served as deputy clerk of the General Court from the 1740s until the Revolution, and he was the clerk of the York County Court from 1745 until his death in 1781.

The Brush-Everard House as originally constructed was a timber-framed one and one-half story building typical of the houses built here in the early years of the eighteenth century. It was covered with weatherboards that were prepared by hand-splitting four-foot lengths of oak boards. The roof was covered with clapboards instead of shingles. A section of the original roofing is still in place, protected over the centuries by the roof ridge of the north addition.

During Everard's tenure the house was enlarged and embellished to reflect the standing of its owner and the changing taste by which a gentleman was judged. The addition of two wings at the back resulted in a U-shaped plan. Fine paneling and rich carving—probably executed by the joiner who worked at Carter's Grove plantation—are evidence of Everard's affluence and taste.

The yard between the house and the outbuildings is paved with the original bricks discovered during the course of archaeological excavations. The wooden

Meet . . . Bristol

Callers at the front door of Thomas Everard's house were greeted by Bristol, Everard's black footman, who was dressed in livery. Bristol's uniform, a respectable suit trimmed with braid and brass buttons, was not as elegant as the livery worn by footmen at the Governor's Palace, however.

In 1768 Everard had purchased Bristol, who was in his late twenties, from the estate of Lieutenant Governor Fauquier. Everard owned other slaves—an elderly groom, two young men who waited on the table and did other chores, and a cook, laundress, and housemaid.

As Everard's manservant, Bristol's main duty was to wait upon his master. In the morning he shaved him and laid out his clothes. At mealtimes he supervised the young men who brought the food to the table and served it. When Everard went out during the day, Bristol usually accompanied him. In the evening he turned down his master's bed, used a bed warmer to take the chill off the sheets, and saw that the fire was well banked for the night.

Bristol was intelligent. He had learned to read (although he could not write), so Everard relied on him to deliver messages, run errands, and purchase provisions for the household. Bristol was proud of his abilities and of the confidence his master placed in him, but he never forgot that he was a slave.

Bristol looked forward to running errands to the Palace. When he had delivered his master's gift of fish and peaches to the governor, the butler had tipped him generously. More importantly, Bristol's trips to the Palace often allowed him a glimpse of Venus, Everard's laundress who had been hired out to work on the governor's staff. Venus always exclaimed at how handsome Bristol looked in his uniform. Occasionally when Bristol had a little free time in the evening, he returned to the Palace scullery where Venus and other black servants gathered. On those occasions Bristol could court her openly. One day soon he planned to ask his master's permission to marry Venus.

McKenzie Apothecary

smokehouse and the brick kitchen are original buildings that have been restored. Everard's slaves lived and worked in these outbuildings.

THE GOVERNOR'S PALACE. A description of the Governor's Palace begins on page 72.

The **Robert Carter House** on the west side of Palace Street was constructed by 1746. It served as the residence of Governor Dinwiddie while the Palace underwent repairs in 1751 and 1752.

The first known owner was Charles Carter, son of Robert "King" Carter, one of the wealthiest Virginians in the colony. Robert Carter Nicholas, another member of the prominent family, purchased it in 1753. Long a leader of the House of Burgesses and treasurer of the colony, Nicholas made it his home until 1761 when he sold the house to his cousin, Councillor Robert Carter.

Robert Carter and his family lived in the house for twelve years. Six of his seventeen children were born here. Finding the dwelling "not sufficiently roomy," the Carters returned to their plantation, called Nomini Hall, in 1773.

The house and the brick outbuilding are original. Other dependencies—including the unusual "breezeway"—were reconstructed.

At mid-century, Dr. Kenneth McKenzie owned and lived on this property with his family. He operated his shop, the **McKenzie Apothecary,** on the site. Dr. McKenzie died in 1755. Among other bequests, he left to his "good friend Doctor James Carter having behaved in a very kind manner to me in my Sickness . . . my Skeleton." Items typical of those sold in the eighteenth century are available in the McKenzie Apothecary.

The **Elkanah Deane House** was named for the Irish coachmaker who paid seven hundred pounds for the original dwelling, shop, and garden on this site in 1772. Deane may have been encouraged to move to Williamsburg from New York by Governor Dunmore. Deane advertised in the *Virginia Gazette* that he "had the Honour of making a Coach, Phaeton, and Chaise, for his Excellency the Right Honourable the Earle of Dunmore."

The same issue of the newspaper carried an advertisement from Joseph Beck, a staymaker in New York City. Beck encouraged the "Ladies of Virginia" to give their orders for stays to Mrs. Deane, who would "take their Measures" and forward them to New York. Beck promised satisfaction.

Tree box topiary and small leaved lindens are conspicuous features of the garden, which is open to the public, behind the Elkanah Deane House.

In the latter part of the eighteenth century, the site of the **Elkanah Deane Shop** was the scene of carriage making on a considerable scale. Wheelwrights, blacksmiths, and harnessmakers were among the artisans who worked together to make carts, wagons, riding chairs, and carriages.

The saddler and harnessmaker was a busy craftsman. Making a saddle—whether a hunt saddle, plantation saddle, hussar saddle, or sidesaddle—tested the

* *Robert Carter House*   *Robert Carter North Quarters*

*** George Wythe House** ⊤

leatherworker's skill. He also produced leather water buckets, fire hoses, inkwells, and helmets, to mention just a few now obsolete products that were common in colonial times.

George Wythe (1726–1806), one of the most influential Americans of his era, lived in the brick **George Wythe House** on the west side of Palace Street. Wythe (pronounced to rhyme with Smith) was born in Elizabeth City County where his father, who died soon after, was a successful planter. Encouraged by his mother, Wythe read widely in the classics, becoming in time perhaps the foremost classical scholar in Virginia. After studying law briefly, he was admitted to the bar at the age of twenty.

Wythe was elected to represent Williamsburg in the House of Burgesses in 1754. He also acted as the colony's attorney general while his friend Peyton Randolph was on a mission in England.

In 1755 Wythe married Elizabeth Taliaferro (pronounced "Tolliver"), daughter of Colonel Richard Taliaferro, who is believed to have designed the Wythe House.

Taliaferro gave the use of the house to his daughter as a wedding present.

The public career of George Wythe spanned a decisive half-century in American life. As close friend and executor of the well-liked royal governors Fauquier and Botetourt, he saw the reputation of

⊤

Elkanah Deane Shop
(*Harnessmaker*)

Leather ranked with iron and wood as one of the most useful natural materials in the eighteenth century. Saddles and harness were much in demand in colonial Virginia, so the saddler-harnessmaker was a busy craftsman indeed.

Elkanah Deane Shop   ⊤

Elkanah Deane House

The career of George Wythe—lawyer, teacher, legislator, and judge—spanned a decisive half-century in American life.

the crown in Virginia at its peak. As a burgess during most of the years from 1754 to 1769, and as clerk of the House from 1769 to 1775, he sided with the patriots in the growing dispute with Parliament. As a legislator and judge during the formation of the young republic, he fought for independence, the protection of individual liberties, and the authority of the courts.

Wythe supported Richard Henry Lee's resolution for independence at Philadelphia, and his name appears first among Virginia signers of the Declaration of Independence. He counseled Virginia to establish a regular army instead of a militia and volunteered for service himself. Instead he was chosen to become speaker of the House of Delegates in 1777, and, in 1778, one of the three judges of Virginia's High Court of Chancery. In consultation with Jefferson and Edmund Pendleton, Wythe aided in revising the laws of Virginia.

This distinguished record of public service was fully matched in importance by Wythe's influence as a teacher and adviser. He probably did more to shape Jefferson's ideas than any other man. Jefferson studied law under Wythe and later referred to him as "my faithful and beloved Mentor in youth, and my most affectionate friend through life."

In 1779 Wythe was appointed to the newly established chair of law at the College of William and Mary, becoming the first individual to hold such a chair in an American university. Among his students was John Marshall, later chief justice of the United States. Wythe resigned his professorship a decade later and, having been appointed judge of the Court of Chancery, moved to Richmond.

Wythe's life ended tragically in 1806. He was poisoned, probably by George Sweeney, a grandnephew who lived with him. In desperate financial straits, Sweeney hoped to profit as the principal beneficiary under his uncle's will. The aged statesman lived on in agony for two weeks, long enough to disinherit his grandnephew. Sweeney was never convicted, primarily because the testimony of a slave, who had witnessed the act, was not then admissible in Virginia courts.

Like many Virginians of his time, Wythe opposed slavery in principle and freed his slaves at his death. He bequeathed his

George Wythe House

The George Wythe House was the home of one of the most distinguished Americans of his era. George Wythe's career as lawyer, burgess and clerk of the House of Burgesses, signer of the Declaration of Independence, framer of the U. S. Constitution, professor of law, and judge spanned more than fifty of the most significant years of this nation's history.

The handsome brick house typifies the larger houses of early Virginia. It features a simple but spacious plan with four rooms and a wide central passage on each floor. In many Virginia houses visitors and servants used the lower passage as a waiting area. During the summer, it became a living room for the family.

Domestic activities—including spinning, weaving, and open hearth cooking—occur seasonally in the Wythe House outbuildings.

"books and small philosophical apparatus" and his "silver cups and goldheaded cane" to his long-time friend, Jefferson.

The Wythe House served as headquarters for Washington just before the siege of Yorktown. Rochambeau occupied it for several months after the surrender of Cornwallis in 1781 while French troops were stationed in Williamsburg.

The Wythe House is spacious but simple in plan. Two rooms on each side flank the large central hall on both the first and second stories. Two great chimneys rise between the paired rooms, thus affording a fireplace in all eight. The smaller windows in the second story have the same number of panes, or "lights," as those on the first floor, a device that increases the apparent size of the house.

Behind the house a symmetrical garden plan divides the property into distinct areas. Archaeological excavations established the locations of major outbuildings in the service yard, which is adjacent to the side street. Among the reconstructed frame dependencies are a smokehouse, kitchen, laundry, lumber house, poultry house, well, dovecote, and stable. The pleasure garden is lined with tree box topiary and ends in an arbor of hornbeam. Two "necessary houses," as privies were called, are nearby. The orchard and the kitchen garden are on the south side of the property.

Shopping Opportunities

MCKENZIE APOTHECARY

Ticket not required

Remedies similar to those that Dr. Kenneth McKenzie purveyed in the mid-eighteenth century are sold in the McKenzie Apothecary. Medicinal herbs, spices, candied ginger, rock candy, and horehound drops are available. The shop also stocks candles of bayberry and beeswax, coffee, tea, pomander balls, clay pipes and tobacco, and soap balls and bars—among other items.

American Express, Mastercard, and Visa credit cards are accepted.

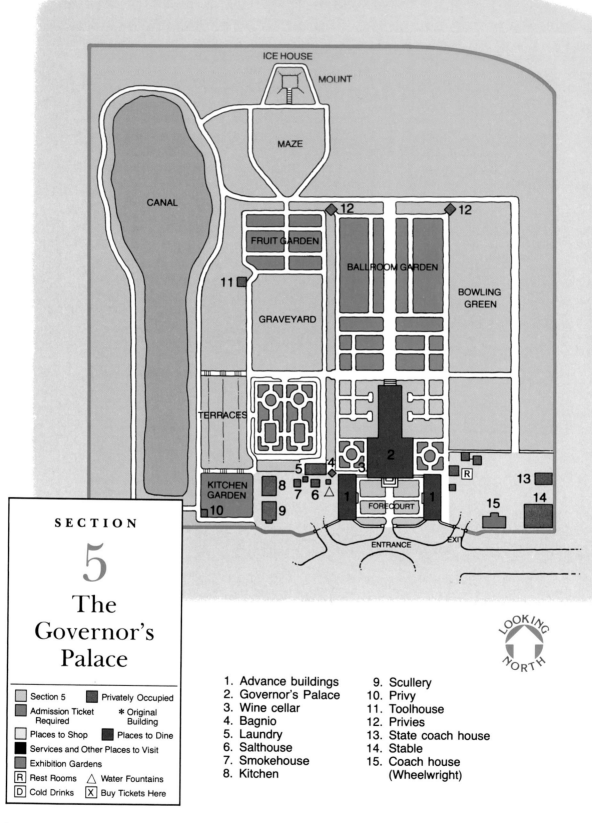

ICE HOUSE

MOUNT

MAZE

CANAL

FRUIT GARDEN

BALLROOM GARDEN

12

12

BOWLING GREEN

11

GRAVEYARD

TERRACES

KITCHEN GARDEN

10

5

4

8

3

2

R

13

7 6

1

1

15

14

9

FORECOURT

ENTRANCE

EXIT

LOOKING NORTH

Section 5

Privately Occupied

Admission Ticket Required

* Original Building

Places to Shop

Places to Dine

Services and Other Places to Visit

Exhibition Gardens

R Rest Rooms

△ Water Fountains

D Cold Drinks

X Buy Tickets Here

1. Advance buildings
2. Governor's Palace
3. Wine cellar
4. Bagnio
5. Laundry
6. Salthouse
7. Smokehouse
8. Kitchen
9. Scullery
10. Privy
11. Toolhouse
12. Privies
13. State coach house
14. Stable
15. Coach house (Wheelwright)

LOOKING NORTH

The Governor's Palace

AT the time of its completion in 1722, the residence of Virginia's royal governor was considered one of the finest such buildings in British America. It is difficult to appreciate just how remarkable this building really was unless the rural character of the colony at the close of the seventeenth century is taken into consideration. In spite of previous attempts to legislate towns into existence, few real towns or centers of commerce existed in Virginia; instead, the colony was populated by widely scattered agricultural settlements that acquired goods through direct trade with shippers and necessary services as needed from rural craftsmen.

The majority of Virginians, even many who were relatively well-to-do, lived in one-story houses composed of no more than two or three rooms. The enclosing walls of these houses often consisted of posts set directly into the earth and given a crude covering of "riven," or split boards. Interior plaster and glass windows were to be found only in houses of the "better sort." By today's standards, living conditions in Virginia at the close of the seventeenth century were modest indeed.

With its broad, straight thoroughfares and its massive public buildings, Williamsburg represented a new beginning—a magnet around which the colony would gather itself and thrive. Unlike most towns in Europe, this new metropolis had been laid out around an orderly ensemble of public buildings related to one another in a grand overall scheme.

The Palace was an important element in this great civic design. Sited at the end of a broad, imposing green, the governor's residence terminated the primary north-south axis of the town. The high visibility and symmetrical formality of this complex did much to elevate the governorship in the eyes of Virginians.

Alexander Spotswood assumed the lieutenant governorship with apparent relish in 1710. More than any other of his contemporaries, Spotswood was determined that the new metropolis (and the governor's house in particular) should affirm the dignity and authority of the colony's educational, religious, and governmental institutions.

Soon after he arrived in Williamsburg, Spotswood set about to effect a series of improvements at the Palace, all of which were intended to amplify its grandeur and enhance his own posture as the crown's appointed representative. The formal vista along Palace Street toward Francis Street, the elaborate gardens with a canal and falling terraces, the enclosed forecourt with its iron gate and royal heraldic beasts, the magnificent display of arms in the entrance hall, and the elegant appointments of the upper middle room where the governor received petitioners were features that appear to have been introduced during Spotswood's time.

From the foot of the green at Duke of Gloucester Street to the inner sanctum of Spotswood's elaborate upper middle room, the Palace complex was a carefully orchestrated procession of spaces moving toward and culminating in the presence of the man sworn to uphold the authority of the English monarch. The architectural setting of the governor's residence was intended to instill in the colonists respect for executive power and prerogative.

The construction of the Governor's Palace began in 1706 during the administration of Lieutenant Governor Edward Nott. In June of that year, following repeated exhortations from the crown, the General Assembly voted to build a residence for the governor and appropriated three thousand pounds toward its erection.

Construction proceeded slowly, however, and the house was little more than an enclosed shell when Spotswood arrived in June 1710. Almost immediately the new governor took charge of the project, pushing it forward vigorously. It was almost certainly at his urging that the Assembly enacted additional legislation providing for the enclosure of the forecourt and gardens and considered further recommendations for "rendering the new House Convenient as well as Ornamental." In October 1711 William Byrd of Westover plantation strolled across town to view the new house, where he saw a magnificent display of weapons in the entrance hall, "nicely posited," as one observer put it, "by the ingenious contrivance of Colonel Spotswood."

Spotswood moved into the house by 1716, although work continued for another six years. In the meantime the governor turned his attention to the gardens where, in the western part, he laid out a series of terraces that descend to a canal below. Before long, however, members of the Assembly expressed alarm at the expenditures being spent for these refinements. In disgust, Spotswood removed himself entirely from any further involvement with the house and grounds.

The house was finally completed by 1722, but it is clear from the journals of the Assembly that minor repairs and even alterations continued to be made on a regular basis. The Palace had fallen into such "ruinous condition" by 1751 that Lieutenant Governor Robert Dinwiddie was forced to take up quarters next door at the house owned by Dr. Kenneth McKenzie (now the Robert Carter House) while extensive repairs were undertaken. By 1752 the Palace had been sufficiently rehabilitated to receive the governor and his household. The real construction work had only begun, however. During the ensuing months, a rear wing encompassing the present ballroom and supper room was erected under the supervision of Richard Taliaferro, who was also responsible for the construction of the George Wythe House.

The creation of two large rooms for public entertainments coincided with the construction of similar spaces elsewhere in Williamsburg. The "great room" at Wetherburn's Tavern, where Governor Dinwiddie was first entertained after taking office, is believed to have been completed about 1750, as was the Apollo Room at the Raleigh Tavern. Such rooms were being added to private residences as well.

The elaborate downstairs room at the Peyton Randolph House appears to date from the same era.

This new desire for large rooms suited to public entertainments echoed a similar trend in England. In 1756 English architect Isaac Ware noted that the addition of a "great room" to private residences had become commonplace, complaining that such an addition "always hangs from one end, or sticks to one side, of the house, and shews to the most careless eye, that, though fastened to the walls it does not belong to the building."

After the completion of the ballroom wing, few changes of any importance oc-

Governor's Palace

The elegant and imposing residence of seven royal governors and the first two governors of the Commonwealth of Virginia—Patrick Henry and Thomas Jefferson—has been reconstructed on its original foundations. In the eighteenth century the Palace served as the residence and official headquarters of the king of England's deputy in the colony.

Within the walls of the recently refurbished Palace are a stable, kitchen, and gardens. The wheelwright demonstrates his craft in the stable area.

Tickets for the Governor's Palace may be obtained at the Visitor Center.

Meet . . .
Governor Francis Fauquier

Francis Fauquier (pronounced "fo-keer") served as lieutenant governor of Virginia from 1758 until he died in Williamsburg on March 3, 1768, at the age of sixty-four. Despite the growing imperial crisis, Fauquier remained a popular and well-respected governor best known for his scientific and humanitarian interests.

When Governor Fauquier was proposed for membership in the Royal Society of London, an organization composed of some of the foremost scientists of the day, he was described as a "Gentleman of great merit, well versed in Philosophical and Mathematical inquiries, and the Advancement of Natural Knowledge." Fauquier's curiosity about things scientific continued in Virginia. His observations in July 1758 about hailstones one and one-half inches long and three-quarters of an inch wide and deep that "broke every pane of glass on the north side of the house and destroyed all the garden things entirely" were summarized in the Royal Society's *Philosophical Transactions*. The day after the storm Governor Fauquier used some of the hailstones to cool wine and freeze cream.

The humane governor urged the Virginia General Assembly to establish a hospital devoted to the mentally ill. In colonial times the care of the insane was left to the vestry of each parish. If the vestry was unable to provide adequate care, the insane either remained at large in a world with which they could not cope or were placed in prison where they might be mistreated. Governor Fauquier therefore directed the attention of the burgesses to the need for better care of "Persons who are so unhappy as to be deprived of their reason." The General Assembly responded by passing an act to "make Provision for the Support and Maintenance of Ideots, Lunaticks, and other Persons of unsound Minds." Opened in 1773, the Public Hospital in Williamsburg was the earliest facility in North America devoted entirely to the care and treatment of the mentally ill.

Because of the great esteem accorded him, Governor Fauquier was buried in the north aisle of Bruton Parish Church. Thomas Jefferson expressed the sentiment of most colonial Virginians when he paid tribute to Fauquier as the "ablest man" who ever filled the office of governor.

---

curred in or around the Palace until the arrival of Norborne Berkeley, Baron de Botetourt, in 1768. Shortly after assuming his post, the governor launched a thorough program of redecoration that is reflected in the furnishings and exterior appointments of the Palace as visitors see it today.

With the coming of the American Revolution, Virginia's last royal governor, John Murray, fourth Earl of Dunmore, fled Williamsburg. The Palace then served as a residence for the first two governors of the new Commonwealth of Virginia, Patrick Henry and Thomas Jefferson. It was probably during his residence in Williamsburg that Jefferson prepared a series of drawings to guide in remodeling the Palace. His proposed changes were never carried out, however, because the seat of government—and the governor's residence—moved to Richmond in 1780.

American forces used the vacant Palace as a hospital following the siege of Yorktown. The orchard terrace overlooking the canal became a burial ground for 156 American soldiers. On the night of December 22, 1781, fire broke out in the Palace and in three hours it had burned to the ground. Shortly afterward all that remained of the central structure's charred hulk was pulled down and the bricks were sold. Within a few short months the once great Palace of Virginia's royal governors had become only a memory, its flanking advance buildings and outlying dependencies tangible reminders of its vanished magnificence.

In the eighteenth century a liveried footman showed callers at the Palace into the entrance hall where the royal coat of arms and ornamental arrangements of weapons represented the authority by which the governor ruled. In England similar arrangements could be seen in the country houses of important men, at the Tower of London, and especially in the guard chambers of royal residences such as Hampton Court and Windsor Castle.

Like those royal guard chambers, the hall at the Palace functioned as a screening area where visitors wishing to see the governor were "sorted out." In the case of Lord Botetourt's household, William Marshman, the butler, supervised this process. Marshman had his office in the pantry to the left of the front door. From this vantage point the butler managed the household staff that consisted of twenty-

The entrance hall to the Governor's Palace.

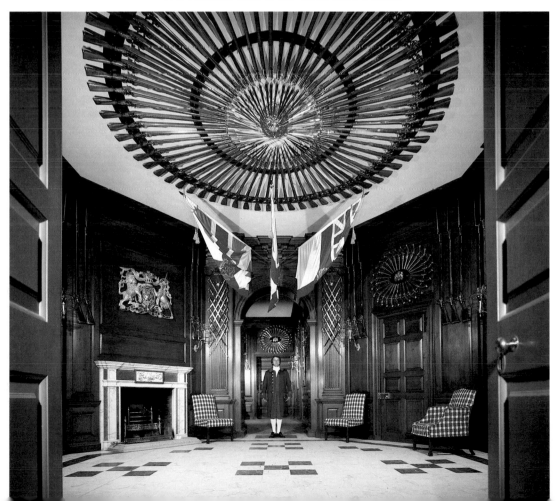

five servants and slaves. Hanging on the door is a ring of keys, a reminder that Marshman also controlled access to the governor's valuable collection of silver and to his stocks of wine and food in the cellar. Beside the library table where household accounts were kept is a bed in which the butler would have slept in order to secure the contents of this important room.

Many if not most visitors would have been shown into the parlor on the right, where they waited their turn with the governor. The serviceable leather upholstery on the chairs in the parlor reflects the role of this space as a waiting room of sorts. Visitors would have found the numerous scripture prints on the walls both entertaining and edifying.

Prominent persons having particularly important business probably proceeded upstairs immediately for an audience with his excellency. Moving through the entry

Meet . . .
William Marshman

William Marshman, butler to Governor Botetourt at the Palace from 1768 to 1770, accompanied his master to Virginia. Marshman had been in his lordship's service for several years, first as a footman and then as a clerk at Stoke Park, Lord Botetourt's residence in England, where his wife, Mary, worked for Lord Botetourt as a housemaid. Like several of Lord Botetourt's servants who traveled to Virginia with him, Marshman left his wife and family behind when he came to Williamsburg in the fall of 1768.

At the Palace Marshman supervised the household staff, which included an under butler, footmen, and housemaids, handled the governor's money, kept the household accounts, and oversaw the serving of meals. He was also responsible for the care and protection of hundreds of pieces of silver and for the contents of the wine cellar. By 1770 Marshman received the highest salary of any member of Governor Botetourt's staff—forty pounds per year plus three pounds to pay for washing his clothes.

Lord Botetourt died in October 1770. For three weeks the devoted butler had waited night and day on his master during his last illness. Marshman's letters to family and friends in England convey his grief, and they also reveal his anxiety about his future.

Botetourt's heir, the fifth Duke of Beaufort, directed that Marshman receive all of his lordship's clothes. Since the late governor had owned—among other items— fifty-six ruffled shirts, thirty-six pairs of shoes, and coats, waistcoats, and britches in a variety of fabrics—black velvet, crimson silk, and gold and silver lace—this was a valuable legacy indeed. Perhaps it eased Marshman's concern somewhat.

"No Servant had ever heaped upon him such continual proof of kindness from any Master," wrote Marshman after Lord Botetourt's death, "as I receiv'd from that Generous and Good Man."

hall and up the wide staircase, they approached the governor's elegant upper middle room, no doubt impressed by the grand procession of spaces with their ornamental displays of firearms and swords. At the head of the stair a visitor might pause expectantly in another waiting area until the time came for him to be received by the governor.

Beyond a final set of doors, the governor himself, amid considerable pomp, received visitors and transacted business, sometimes while his servants dressed him, in the elaborately appointed middle room. Strange as it may sound today, this ceremony, called a "levee," was a customary practice in Europe among men of power and influence. No doubt such levees effectively portrayed the governor of colonial Virginia as a dignified and potent leader.

Those who enjoyed a close friendship with the governor might be invited into his bedchamber on the right, or, in the case of his most intimate associates, into the library beyond it. Because Lord Botetourt was a bachelor, he is likely to have designated the two bedchambers on the east for the use of visiting dignitaries such as Governor and Mrs. William Tryon of North Carolina, guests at the Palace in June 1769.

Not everyone calling at the Palace sought a private audience with the governor. Many attended him in his dining room, an area dedicated as much to business and politics as to meals. Lord Botetourt's dining room contained such clerical necessities as a small reading desk, a library table, and a mahogany desk that held public and private papers.

The governor's dining room was a male enclave from which ladies typically withdrew after meals, leaving the men to their bottles. In some cases the decor of dining rooms in colonial Virginia reflected their masculine character. At Mt. Airy, for example, Colonel John Tayloe covered the dining room walls with portraits of English racehorses.

Food was kept warm in the little middle room before being taken into the dining room across the passage. During mealtimes this area bustled with activity.

Many visitors arrived at the Palace to enjoy the governor's entertainments. From the entrance hall guests passed through the set of double doors leading into the ballroom, where dances or "routs" (as those occasions were sometimes called) took place.

Among the most fashionable and up-to-date rooms in the building, the ballroom and supper room became a stage on which the governor and his guests acted out the latest forms of etiquette and displayed themselves as being in touch with the world's most fashionable and civilized conversation and manners. Early in the eighteenth century such an event would have involved a relatively small group of people, all engaged in a single activity in one room. Later in the century, however, assemblies

A glass pyramid dressed for the dessert course graces the table in the Palace dining room.

included many more guests and featured a variety of activities going on in separate rooms. While people danced in one room, refreshments or a light supper might be served in another.

At the far end of the supper room a last pair of doors leads visitors into a formal garden resembling those found on many English estates during the early eighteenth century. Quite often those formal gardens served to frame pleasing views of distant pastoral scenery. This distant landscape, called a park, was in many cases planted with clumps of trees arranged informally for a picturesque effect. Grazing cattle or a herd of deer usually completed the scene. By providing pleasing prospects, or vistas, to be enjoyed from near the house, the park functioned as an important adjunct to the formal garden.

Just such a park, which encompassed sixty-three acres, complemented the governor's gardens. Like many of its English counterparts, this park was visible from a mount in the formal garden or as visitors looked northward through the delicate tracery of the great wrought-iron gate. Governor Botetourt made occasional excursions into the park, enjoying its idyllic beauty from a special horse-drawn vehicle called a park-chair. Governor Dunmore seems to have favored the park for morning walks.

The formal garden with its manicured parterres was equally important as a source of pleasurable recreation. Here gentlemen might stroll along fragrant walks, trading pleasant flatteries with the ladies, or perhaps continuing a conversation begun over dinner. Above all, however, these impressive gardens helped to present the governor as a refined and important man. In this respect they functioned as an extension of the house and mirrored its formal character.

Farther from the house, in the westernmost part of the garden, Spotswood's terraces, planted in a less formal manner than the rest of the garden, fall gently to the fish pond below. Spotswood capitalized on the topographic variety of the site, an approach to gardening that gained favor in England as designers began to move away from the rigid formality of an earlier age.

The stables and carriage house in the east yard served the transportation needs of the household. Lord Botetourt's state coach, a heavily gilded ceremonial vehicle in which the governor rode to the Capitol to open sessions of the General Assembly, was kept in the coach house. The elegance of his excellency's coach led one visitor to comment on the tendency of Virginians

Wheelwright

In the eighteenth century there was a demand for wheeled vehicles of every kind. Wheelbarrows, riding chairs, carriages, and carts—all were needed to move people or possessions from place to place. Wheeled vehicles of every description could be seen in the streets of Virginia's colonial capital.

A good bit of basic geometry goes into the making of a wheel, a perfect wooden circle into which the spokes—usually twelve or fourteen in number—are mortised. After an iron rim, or tire, is fitted into place, the wheel is ready to roll.

"to adopt ideas of royalty and magnificence."

These service yards were also the centers of social life for the governor's household staff and, as such, while less elegant than the ballroom, they were no less important.

The service yards are located to the east and west of the advance buildings that flank the Palace. The elegance of the governor's residence did not just happen; it was the product of hard work by many servants—butlers, footmen, cooks, laundresses, maids, gardeners, grooms, and laborers. The kitchen, scullery, and laundry, along with other support buildings involved in the task of maintaining the household, are in the west yard. Of special interest is the hexagonal "bagnio" or bathhouse, a luxury rarely found elsewhere in Virginia. The butler had direct access to this entire service area by way of the mansion's west door.

Meet . . . James

Royal governors Fauquier, Botetourt, and Dunmore in turn hired James, a slave from Carter's Grove plantation, to work in the gardens at the Governor's Palace. They paid the Burwell family twelve pounds a year from 1765 through 1771 for James's services.

James was highly regarded for his practical knowledge of gardening. He had learned how to use bell glasses, hot beds, and other methods for forcing plants from Christopher Ayscough, Governor Fauquier's head gardener. James also knew how to prune fruit trees and how to transplant native seedlings successfully.

James occasionally received tips from visitors to the Palace. He might have spent these small sums on ribbons for his daughters, on fowl that his wife could raise, or on rum for himself.

James's wife, Betty, and their three children lived on the plantation. The black cooper at Carter's Grove was teaching Juba, fifteen, to make barrels. In the eighteenth century barrels and kegs of various shapes and sizes were the common containers for storing and shipping all kinds of goods. Phebee, age thirteen, helped her mother in the kitchen. Eight-year-old Jenny ran errands. On Saturday evenings James would usually "night walk" the eight miles to Carter's Grove so that he could spend Sunday with his family.

On Sundays James cultivated a garden plot at his family's quarter that supplied vegetables to supplement the food rations his wife and children received. It is likely, too, that he found time on this day of rest to divert and entertain himself with kinfolk, neighbors, and friends.

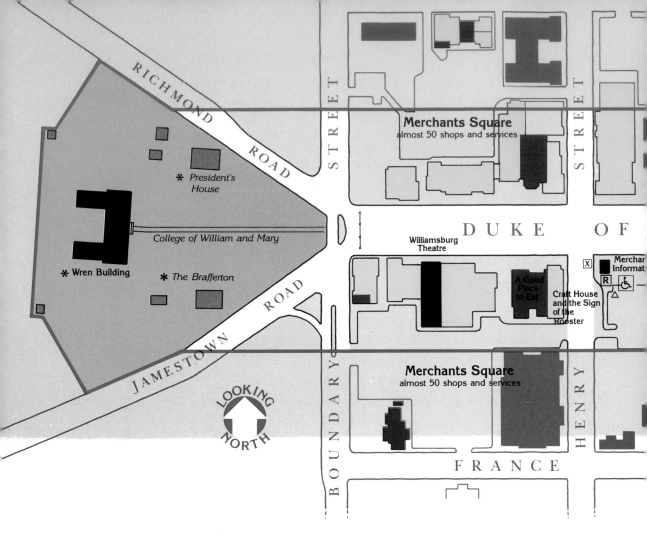

Merchants Square
almost 50 shops and services

* President's
House

College of William and Mary

* Wren Building

* The Brafferton

RICHMOND ROAD

JAMESTOWN ROAD

STREET

STREET

DUKE OF

Williamsburg
Theatre

A Good
Piece
to Eat

Craft House
and the Sign
of the
Rooster

Merchant
Informat

Merchants Square
almost 50 shops and services

BOUNDARY

FRANCE

HENRY

LOOKING NORTH

From Palace Street to the College of William and Mary

FOR most of the seventeenth century what is now Williamsburg was little more than a winding horsepath faced by a tavern, a few stores, and several houses. Two important institutions fostered the growth of this part of the street. The first, Bruton Parish Church, was located here in 1674. The second, the colony's new College named to honor King William and Queen Mary of England, was chartered in 1693. These two institutions,

less than a half-mile apart, drew workers, artisans, and businessmen to Middle Plantation, the sparsely settled outpost that had been established in 1633 on the ridge between the James and York rivers.

The appeal of locating the center of government near the colony's center of learning was partly responsible for the General Assembly's choice in 1699 of Middle Plantation as the site of the new capital. In practical terms, the great hall at the Col-

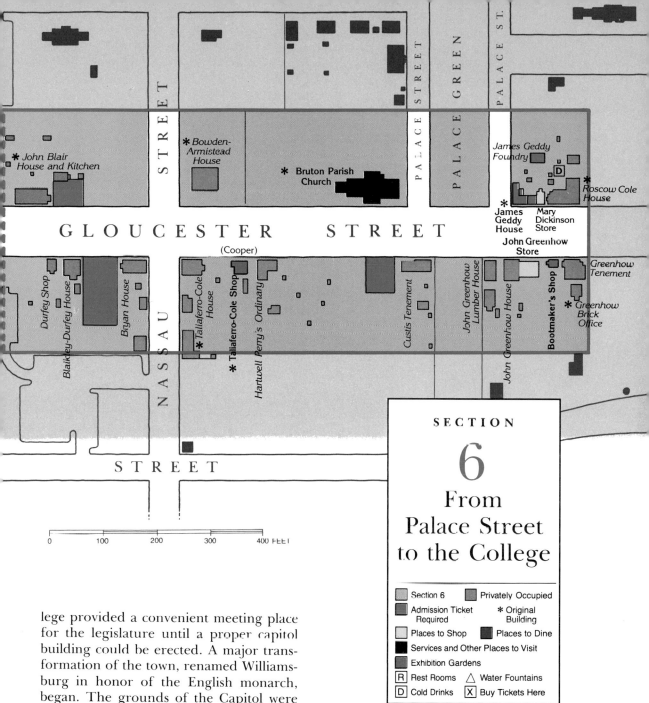

Map labels

* John Blair
House and Kitchen

* Bowden-
Armistead
House

* Bruton Parish
Church

James Geddy
Foundry

Roscow Cole
House

* James
Geddy
House

Mary
Dickinson
Store

John Greenhow
Store

STREET

PALACE STREET

PALACE GREEN

PALACE ST.

GLOUCESTER STREET

(Cooper)

Durfey Shop

Blaikley-Durfey House

Bryan House

Taliaferro-Cole
House

* Taliaferro-Cole Shop

Hartwell Perry's Ordinary

Custis Tenement

John Greenhow
Lumber House

John Greenhow House

Bootmaker's Shop

Greenhow
Tenement

* Greenhow
Brick
Office

N A S S A U

STREET

STREET

| 0 | 100 | 200 | 300 | 400 FEET |

lege provided a convenient meeting place for the legislature until a proper capitol building could be erected. A major transformation of the town, renamed Williamsburg in honor of the English monarch, began. The grounds of the Capitol were located about a mile east of the College, with Duke of Gloucester Street linking the two buildings. The old path was widened and straightened, and any buildings standing in the new roadway were removed.

This "uptown" section of Williamsburg took on a more residential appearance than the busier "downtown" blocks of Duke of Gloucester Street near the Capitol. After the government moved to Rich-

mond in 1780, commercial activity at the eastern end of the street declined. The College and the Public Hospital became Williamsburg's major local institutions, and the focus of town life shifted back to this part of the city.

LOOKING NORTH

* ***James Geddy House*** 🆃   *Mary Dickinson*
   and Foundry   *Store*

From Palace Street to Nassau Street

From about 1737 to 1777, gunsmith James Geddy and his sons lived at or operated shops on the site of the ***James Geddy House*** and ***James Geddy Workshop and Kitchen***. A good deal more than gunsmithing went on here, however. An inventory taken after James Geddy's death lists shop equipment, including brasswork for guns, a turner's lathe, bullet molds, and gunsmith's, cutler's, and founder's tools. In 1751 Geddy's sons David and William advertised that they were carrying on these trades at the shop near the church.

In 1760 the widowed Anne Geddy sold the property to her son James, Jr., who set up shop as a silversmith, goldsmith, and watch repairer. He also sold and repaired jewelry and objects of silver. It was difficult to attract customers to a location so far away from the busy Capitol. In a 1771 advertisement a concerned Geddy hoped that the reasonableness of his prices would "remove the Objection of his Shop's being too high up Town . . . and the Walk may be thought rather an Amusement than a Fatigue."

🆃

James Geddy House and Foundry

The James Geddy House was the eighteenth-century home, workshop, and shop of a successful family of artisans. The domestic and commercial activities of the family of James Geddy, Jr., are interpreted in the house today.

In the foundry behind the house, skilled craftsmen cast useful objects of beauty in bronze, brass, pewter, and silver.

William Waddill, a journeyman silversmith and engraver, worked in Geddy's shop. In 1770 Waddill made eight silver handles, sixteen escutcheons, and a large engraved nameplate for Governor Botetourt's coffin. James Geddy married Elizabeth Waddill, who probably was William's sister. A leader in the community, James Geddy was one of three artisans named to the Williamsburg common council.

The two-story L-shaped Geddy house dates from the 1760s. Its low-pitched roof without dormers and the front porch with balcony and doorway above are unusual features.

The Geddys operated a foundry behind the house. In the eighteenth century the yard around several busy forges would have been littered with piles of coal, mounds of slag, and assorted iron and brass waste.

Mary Dickinson advertised millinery, jewelry, and other goods for sale "next Door to MR. JAMES GEDDY'S Shop, near the Church" in an October 1771 issue of the *Virginia Gazette.* Today an elegant assortment of items is again available in the **Mary Dickinson Store.**

The frame **Greenhow Tenement,** across and down the street from the Geddy House, was once the property of John Greenhow, whose son sold it to printer and newspaper publisher Joseph Repiton in 1810.

In 1773 George Wilson & Company advertised the arrival of a "choice Cargo of the best sorts of English Leather for all Manner of Mens Shoes and Pumps" at the **Boot and Shoemaker's Shop.** Wilson must have had more business than he could handle since he encouraged two or three journeymen shoemakers to apply to him "next Door to Mr. Greenhow's Store in Williamsburg." By the end of the next year, however, the household furniture and working materials of George Wilson, deceased, were offered for sale.

Boot and Shoemaker's Shop

Today a craftsman again makes shoes using the tools and techniques of the eighteenth century. He hand sews the soles and uppers with "good thread well twisted" and stitches that are "hard drawn with handleathers" as one colonial Virginia statute prescribed.

An eighteenth-century shoemaker could turn out an average of two pairs of shoes per day. He made them with round, square, or pointed toes as fashion might decree, although he generally used a straight last—that is, without distinction between right and left—because gentlemen felt that straight shoes presented a more pleasing appearance.

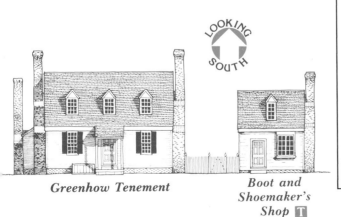

Greenhow Tenement

Boot and Shoemaker's Shop T

John Greenhow Store

Ticket not required

From the merchant's counting room in back to the freshly painted sign above the front door, John Greenhow's Store is an authentic re-creation of its eighteenth-century counterpart. Advertisements in the *Virginia Gazette* from 1766 to 1780 enabled researchers to identify the wide variety of goods that John Greenhow and his sons sold in their general store. Wrought iron, willow baskets, fine imported porcelain, floorcloths, fabrics, cooper's items, tinware, craftsmen's tools and supplies, "and almost every other useful article that can be thought of" are featured again today.

One contemporary account described the home of John Greenhow, a merchant in Williamsburg from about 1755 to his death in 1787, as "a large and commodious Dwelling House." The adjoining *John Greenhow Store* is the most completely reconstructed eighteenth-century commercial space in Williamsburg. Viewed from the street, the building appears to be in three segments. From left to right, there is a sloped-roof counting room and office for the proprietor, the entrance to the store, and the doorway to the *John Greenhow House.* The separate building to the right whose gable end faces the street is the *John Greenhow Lumber House.* It functioned as a stockroom for furniture, barrels, and odds and ends too bulky to keep in the store itself. In eighteenth-century parlance the term "lumber" meant, essentially, "items in storage."

The generous size, layout, and exterior finish of the combination store and home and the lumber house are indicated on several early nineteenth-century fire insurance policies taken out by Greenhow's son Robert. The insurance plats also show that behind the Greenhow property the slope of the ravine—with its meadows, gardens, corn house, and other outbuildings—was put to an agricultural use typical of lots at this end of Duke of Gloucester Street.

The *Custis Tenement* stands on a lot that John Custis acquired in 1714. Custis also purchased two lots to the immediate west,

John Greenhow Store and House   *John Greenhow Lumber House*

Meet . . .
John Greenhow

According to his tombstone in Bruton churchyard, Greenhow was born November 12, 1724, and died August 29, 1787. Raised in Westmoreland County, England, he may be the same John Greenhow whose bankruptcy in nearby Lancaster, England, was announced in a 1752 issue of the *Universal Magazine*.

Greenhow's name first appeared in Virginia records about that time. By the 1760s newspaper advertisements show that his house and store were located on Duke of Gloucester Street across from the Geddy property.

John Greenhow was an enterprising and far-ranging merchant. His eight-ton, three-man schooner, the *Robert*, regularly plied between the James River and Philadelphia, carrying peas, pork, lard, and butter northward. The return journey brought earthenware, flour, bread, bar iron, chocolate, coffee, iron skillets, saddletrees, soap, and furniture such as chairs, tables, and chests of drawers. He even operated a second store in Richmond.

Advertisements that listed the variety of imported goods stocked by John Greenhow appeared regularly in the *Virginia Gazette*, most especially before sessions of the General Court and the Court of Oyer and Terminer, which brought large numbers of people to town. Greenhow's stated policy of selling for "ready money only" was probably intended just for nonresidents. Had his account books survived, they undoubtedly would show that he occasionally sold goods to townspeople on credit.

---

built structures on them, and rented the properties as tenements. Cabinetmaker Peter Scott's residence, for example, was located in the open lot west of the formal garden.

Custis Tenement

In 1746 Custis leased a house on this lot to carpenter John Wheatley for three years, during which time Wheatley was to maintain the house in good repair and "continually to keep the Chimneys clean swept for fear of fire." He continued to rent the property through 1757, according to accounts presented in court by Martha Custis, the widow of Daniel Parke Custis who had inherited the property from his father. The widow Custis later married George Washington.

Just as English and European towns and villages had for centuries grown up around parish churches, so too did Middle Plantation. The tombs, gravestones, and site of a modest brick church completed in 1683 are reminders of the small seventeenth-century hamlet that was transformed into Williamsburg by Governor Nicholson's plan for a new city designed to be a fit seat for the colonial capital of Virginia.

In the late seventeenth century, before the College was built, **Bruton Parish Church** was the most important public building at Middle Plantation. Named for a town in Somerset, England, Bruton Parish was established here in 1674 when several smaller parishes were joined together. Three years later, the vestry ordered that a church be built on the site. A small buttressed brick church was completed in 1683. Francis Louis Michel, a Swiss traveler who visited Williamsburg in 1702, left a sketch of the first Bruton Parish Church which shows that it had curvilinear end gables done in the Flemish manner. Its foundations are marked by granite posts northwest of the present church.

The small church was badly in need of repair by the early 1700s. Furthermore, it could not accommodate the many people who came to Williamsburg during "Publick Times" when the courts were convened. The vestrymen therefore petitioned the General Assembly "for their Generous contribution" toward building a new church. Lieutenant Governor Alexander Spotswood, an architectural enthusiast, provided a "platt or draught of the Church" and the Assembly appropriated two hundred pounds toward the cost. Begun in 1712, the cruciform Bruton Church has been in continuous use since 1715.

James Morris, carpenter, supervised the construction of Bruton Church. Other Williamsburg artisans also worked on the structure; for example, Lewis Delony built the original pews.

The chancel was extended twenty-five feet to the east in 1752, and an English organ was installed in 1755. In 1769 local contractor Benjamin Powell was awarded

* *Bruton Parish Church*

the contract to build a new tower and steeple. The much darker shade of the bricks used in the tower contrasts with the soft salmon color of the brickwork of the main building. The bell, given to the parish by merchant James Tarpley in 1761, is still in use today.

From 1903 to 1907, under the direction of then rector Dr. W. A. R. Goodwin, the church was stripped of nineteenth-century changes in an effort to return the interior to the way it had looked in the 1700s. A more complete restoration occurred in 1940.

The churchyard was surrounded by a brick wall in 1754. Many graves are located in the churchyard, although in the eighteenth century it was more often the custom for people to be buried at home in private cemeteries. The Reverend Hugh Jones complained about this custom in 1724 because it meant he had to travel long distances to officiate at burials. Typical private plots can be seen today behind the Custis Tenement and the Taliaferro-Cole House across the street. Some of the table tombs in the Bruton churchyard were imported from England.

Made up of twelve men, the vestry regulated church affairs and imposed whatever annual taxes it thought necessary to pay the minister's salary, provide relief for the poor of the parish, and repair the church. The Anglican church was supported by the state in colonial Virginia, and every white (except for a few Quakers who formally dissented and some Catholics) was deemed a member, had to attend divine services at least once each month, and could be fined for failure to attend. All officeholders were obliged to conform to the established church, and all taxpayers, regardless of religious preference, were expected to support it and participate in its sacraments.

Divine services were held each Sunday morning. They included readings from the Book of Common Prayer, a sermon, and, four times a year, the taking of holy communion. Services were also held on Christmas Day and Good Friday.

Blacks living in the parish also worshipped at Bruton Church. Scores of

Bruton Parish Church
Ticket not required; admission by donation

Bruton Parish Church, an Episcopal church in continuous use since 1715, is a reminder of the part religion played in the lives of eighteenth-century Virginians at a time when church and state were united.

The walls and windows are original, as is the west gallery where students at the College sat. The initials they carved in the handrail are still discernible. Tradition has it that the stone baptismal font was brought from an earlier church at Jamestown.

In colonial days it was considered to be an honor to be buried within the church. Among the graves in Bruton Parish Church is that of royal governor Francis Fauquier.

LOOKING NORTH

* *Bowden-Armistead House*

slaves—who sat apart in the north gallery—attended Sunday services. After the mid-eighteenth century, more than one thousand slaves, many of them infants, were baptized in Bruton Church. Inspired by two black preachers, Gowan Pamphlet and Moses, a number of black parishioners established a church of their own after the Revolution. With a membership of five hundred, "the Baptist Church of black people at Williamsburg" was received into the Dover Baptist Association in 1793. The site of their church, on Nassau Street opposite the Taliaferro-Cole stable, is marked by a plaque.

The ***Bowden-Armistead House,*** completed in 1858 of Baltimore stock brick, is a good example of Greek Revival architectural taste. It is surrounded by an iron fence brought from Richmond.

Lemuel J. Bowden, a lawyer and president of the board of overseers of Eastern State Hospital, purchased the land on which the house stands from Bruton Parish Church. Town residents—including his mother—considered Bowden, one of Williamsburg's few Northern sympathizers during the Civil War, to be a traitor and

Taliaferro-Cole Shop T
(*Cooper*)

The Taliaferro-Cole Shop houses the craft of coopering. In the eighteenth century barrels and kegs of various sizes and shapes were the common containers for storing, carrying, and shipping all kinds of goods—from flour and tobacco to boots and brandy.

Staves split from white oak are formed into a circle, held in place by trussing rings, finally shaped by heat and iron hoops, and given a tight-fitting, flat head. The products of the cooper's trade may be standardized and utilitarian, yet they are beautiful in their shapes and proportions.

LOOKING SOUTH

Hartwell Perry's Ordinary

* *Taliaferro-Cole Shop* T

* *Taliaferro-Cole House*

gave him the unflattering sobriquet of "Virginia Yankee."

Hartwell Perry's Ordinary was named for Hartwell Perry, who owned and operated an ordinary, as colonial taverns were sometimes called, on the site from the mid-1780s until he died about 1800. Earlier the land had been owned by John Custis, who built yet another tenement on the property and rented it in 1746 to joiner and cabinet-maker James Spiers.

The sign hanging out front is a rebus. It depicts a deer, a well, and several pears. "Hart" is another name for a deer, and an alcoholic beverage made from pears is called "perry"—so the sign stands for Hartwell Perry.

Despite a late nineteenth-century facade and earlier additions to the rear, the original **Taliaferro-Cole Shop** had remained essentially intact when the building was acquired for restoration. Charles Taliaferro (pronounced "Tolliver") built the shop sometime before 1782. In 1804 Jesse Cole purchased the shop and the house next door. He used the shop as a post office and general store. Today the shop houses the craft of the cooper.

From at least 1724 until his death in 1756, Thomas Crease, gardener at the College and Palace at various times, and his wife owned and lived on the lot where the **Taliaferro-Cole House** is located today. In a newspaper advertisement of 1738, Crease announced that he had ornamental plants for sale. He may have used part of this lot as a nursery. If so, it would have added to the pastoral appearance of the western end of Williamsburg.

By the 1770s coachmaker Charles Taliaferro owned this lot. Taliaferro operated a store "opposite the church wall."

From Nassau Street to Merchants Square

A gable-roofed house probably built sometime after mid-century on the present site of the **Bryan House** survived until the twentieth century. At different times it served as a grocery store, residence, and school.

William Blaikley and his wife, Catherine, lived in the **Blaikley-Durfey House** next door. When he died in 1736, William bequeathed "unto my loving wife Catherine Blaikley, all my whole estate of lands, houses, negroes, goods, and chattels."

Catherine, who apparently never remarried, remained at this address until her death in 1771 at the age of seventy-three. A remarkable woman, she was renowned as an "eminent Midwife . . . who, in the course of her Practice, brought upwards of three thousand Children into the World."

In April 1773 tailor Severinus Durfey announced his move to the house formerly occupied by Mrs. Blaikley. He used the **Durfey Shop** to the west for his tailoring activities and for other commercial pur-

LOOKING SOUTH

Bryan House   *Blaikley-Durfey House*   *Durfey Shop*

* *John Blair House and Kitchen*

poses. The golden fleece of the signboard is the traditional symbol of a tailor's shop.

The *John Blair House and Kitchen* on the north side of Duke of Gloucester Street was the home of a prominent family of Virginians. The Reverend James Blair (1655–1743), founder and first president of the College of William and Mary, came to Virginia in 1685. His brother, Dr. Archibald Blair, arrived in 1690. Archibald's son, John Blair, Sr., received a legacy of ten thousand pounds from his uncle James, who left his library and five hundred pounds to the College.

John Blair, Sr. (1689–1771), a burgess and auditor general of the colony from 1728 to 1771, was appointed to the Council in 1745. Later, as president of the Council, he twice served as acting governor of the colony. His son, John Blair, Jr. (1732–1800), graduated from William and Mary and studied law at the Middle Temple in London. He was elected to the House of Burgesses and later became clerk of the Council. He sat on the committee that drew up Virginia's Declaration of Rights and first state constitution, and he served the new commonwealth as councillor, judge, and chief justice. In 1787 he represented Virginia at the Constitutional Convention, where he firmly advocated federal union, and in 1789 President George Washington appointed him to the United States Supreme Court.

The original, easterly part of the John Blair House was built early in the eighteenth century. It is one of the oldest

houses in Williamsburg. Town tradition has it that the stone steps at both doors came from the Palace Street theater. The steps were added when the house was lengthened twenty-eight feet to the west sometime during the second quarter of the eighteenth century.

The kitchen, with its huge chimney, has been reconstructed. Between the kitchen and the street is a small formal herb garden that is open to the public.

The 1782 Frenchman's Map shows quite a few buildings on the last block of Duke of

Meet . . . Anne Blair and Her Niece, Betsey Braxton

Anne Blair was twenty-three in 1769. The daughter of John Blair, Sr., she was his next to youngest child and only remaining unmarried daughter. Anne lived with her father and her brother John and his family in the John Blair House on Duke of Gloucester Street. As the charming—and unattached—daughter of a well-to-do family, Anne garnered quite a few admirers and enjoyed an almost constant round of balls and other social gatherings.

Anne arranged to have her niece, Betsey Braxton, spend the summer of 1769 in Williamsburg. Anne supervised ten-year-old Betsey's reading and sewing, took her on afternoon visits and to dancing lessons, and, when necessary, disciplined her.

Anne described their activities in a letter to Betsey's mother: "Bettsey is well, and begs her Duty to you . . . tomarrow is Dancing day, for it is in her thoughts by Day and her dreams by Night. Mr. Fearson [the dancing master] was surprized to find she knew so much of the Minuet step."

Later that summer, while Anne spent a week visiting friends and attending balls in Hampton, her sister-in-law Jean Blair took over Betsey's care. Jean reported that "I had only occasion to Scold her once; and she own'd her falt and seem'd very sorry for it, and Promised never to do so again."

Gloucester Street, an area that is now called **Merchants Square,** but little is known about the people who resided there or the structures in which they lived. Usually a tavern and other businesses catered to the needs of the faculty and students at the College.

Merchants Square Information Station, at the corner of South Henry and Duke of Gloucester streets, is open daily for information and admission tickets.

Today Merchants Square is again a busy commercial and shopping district. The stores are modeled after eighteenth- and early nineteenth-century structures from Maryland and Delaware. Almost fifty years old, Merchants Square is one of the first planned shopping centers in America.

The orderly and almost symmetrical area of the **College of William and Mary** yard at the western end of Duke of Gloucester Street forms an architectural unit in itself. The central structure is the **Wren Building** with its massive chimneys and lofty cupola. Flanking it to the north and south are the **President's House** and

The Brafferton, buildings apparently identical to one another in dimension and detail, although The Brafferton is actually somewhat smaller. The narrow, many paned windows and steeply pitched roofs of these two buildings give a strong vertical accent to the architectural composition.

The College of William and Mary is the second oldest institution of higher education in the United States. It received a charter from King William and Queen Mary in 1693 after the General Assembly sent the Reverend James Blair to England to persuade the royal couple to found an Anglican college so that "the Church of Virginia may be furnish'd with a Seminary of Ministers of the Gospel." The College was also established in order "that the Youth may be piously educated in good Letters and Manners, and the Christian Faith may be propagated amongst the Western Indians, to the Glory of Almighty God."

In the eighteenth century a higher education was not easily acquired in the colonies, so the few who attained it enjoyed considerable prestige. Plantation owners commonly entrusted their young sons to tutors who lived with the family. Occasionally a few studied with a clergyman who augmented his income by running a small school. Young men then obtained a higher education by attending the College of William and Mary or going overseas to study at the universities of Oxford, Cambridge, or Edinburgh. Some read law at the Inns of Court in London.

Students at the College of William and Mary received a classical education. The grammar school admitted boys of about twelve who prepared for college level work by mastering Latin and Greek as well as mathematics, geography, and penmanship. Latin was the language of both written and spoken classwork.

In addition to logic, rhetoric, and ethics, older students studied natural philosophy—mathematics, physics, and metaphysics. After four years of study in the school of

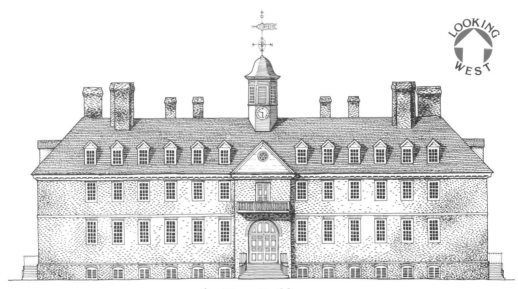

*   *Wren Building*

philosophy, young men who submitted a written thesis and made a successful oral defense of it were awarded a Bachelor of Arts degree. Most students at the College in the eighteenth century left without taking a degree, however.

The faculty included such distinguished men as the Reverend Hugh Jones, mathematician and grammarian, Dr. William Small, physicist, and George Wythe, jurist and classics teacher. "I know of no place in the world," wrote Jefferson in 1788, "while the present professors remain, where I would so soon place a son."

It was largely through the influence of alumnus Jefferson that the curriculum was broadened in 1779. To the old professorships of moral philosophy, natural philosophy, and mathematics were added new chairs of law and police, chemistry and medicine, ethics and belles lettres, and modern languages. The chair of divinity and the grammar school were discontinued. William and Mary had been founded as an Anglican college but, as the Reverend James Madison, then president of the College, explained, "It is now thought that Establishments in favor of any particular Sect are incompatible with the Freedom of a Republic."

The Wren Building bears the name of the distinguished English architect, Sir Christopher Wren, who may possibly have influenced its original design. Construction began in 1695. The building's front and its north wing, which contains a great hall, were completed by 1700. The chapel wing was added in 1732. Although fires in 1705, 1859, and 1862 did serious damage, the massive exterior walls of the Wren Building are largely original. They have withstood not only flames but also the architectural modifications and structural alterations that were part of each rebuilding. The Wren Building now has the outward appearance that it showed from early in the eighteenth century until the fire of 1859.

The courtyard was originally intended to be enclosed within a quadrangular building, the two wings being joined across the far ends by a structure similar to the front side. Jefferson, an accomplished amateur architect, drew plans for an enlarged quadrangle, and foundations had been laid when the outbreak of the Revolution put an end to the project. Some of those foundations still exist.

The president, the professors, and the master of the grammar school ate at the head table in the great hall, the dining room for the College. At the other tables, in descending order of status, sat the students, lesser faculty, "servitors and college officers," and finally the Indian master and his pupils. From the kitchen, directly below, the housekeeper saw to it that "plenty of Victuals" were "served up in the cleanest and neatest Manner possible" three times each day.

The House of Burgesses met in the great hall during the years 1700 to 1704 while the Capitol was under construction. The government of Governor Nicholson crowded all of its activities and offices into the building, "to the great disturbance of the College business," President Blair complained. The burgesses met there again from 1747 to 1754 while the Capitol was rebuilt after being gutted by fire.

Added in 1732, the chapel is evidence that in colonial Virginia the established Church of England played a central role in education as well as in government. In the crypt below the chapel are buried Sir John Randolph, his sons Peyton and John, Governor Botetourt, Bishop James Madison, and several other distinguished Virginians.

Students began the day at 6 or 7 o'clock with morning prayer service in the chapel. Classes were held in the morning and again after midday dinner. Evening prayer or evensong was said at 5 P.M. A light supper followed, and the day ended when the whole student body gathered before the masters to be counted, blessed, and sent to bed.

The second floor common room, where the professors and masters gathered to converse and relax, would today be called the faculty lounge or library. The president and masters met in the convocation room, familiarly known to generations of students as the "blue room," to conduct

Wren Building
Ticket not required

The foundations of the Wren Building, the oldest academic building still in use in America, were laid in 1695. Throughout the colonial period the College of William and Mary was the center of higher education in Virginia. It is the second oldest college in the United States.

Although the average enrollment during the eighteenth century was less than one hundred, the College of William and Mary greatly influenced the intellectual life of Virginia and produced an extraordinary number of distinguished alumni, including Thomas Jefferson, John Marshall, and James Monroe.

The Wren Building was the first major Williamsburg structure to be restored by John D. Rockefeller, Jr.

Meet . . .
Walker Maury

The Botetourt Medal features a portrait of George III on one side and the Reverend James Blair receiving the charter of the College of William and Mary from their majesties on the other.

Born in 1752, Walker Maury attended the grammar school and then graduated from the College of William and Mary in 1775. He capped his distinguished college career by winning one of the prestigious Botetourt Medals for excellence in the classics.

Maury was active in the F. H. C. Society, a forerunner of the fraternity system, which had been organized at William and Mary in 1750. No one knows the secret of the Latin words represented by the letters "F. H. C." In their correspondence with one another, members always called it the "F. H. C. Society," although they specifically mentioned their devotion to friendship, mirth and conviviality, science, and charity.

Shortly after graduating from William and Mary, Maury gave a party for several of his fellow students at a local tavern. The students stayed at the tavern until "one of them at least was in Liquor." Since they had failed to obtain permission for a late evening, when they returned they found the front door of the College locked. The group created such a disturbance trying to get in that the faculty investigated their behavior. Maury took the blame. Taking into account his record of previous good behavior, the faculty found Maury guilty of "a single Act of Intemperance into which he was betray'd by an harmless design to give an Entertainment to some of his fellow Students on his departure from the College" and required him to apologize to the professor who had been disturbed by the rowdy group.

Maury later established a grammar school in the old Capitol.

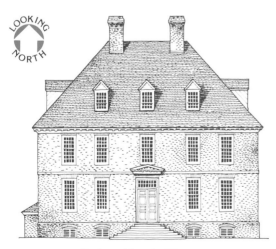

LOOKING NORTH

* *President's House*

College business. They summoned students to the blue room to be commended or censured for their academic—or occasionally for their extracurricular—behavior.

Built in 1732–1733, the ***President's House*** has been the residence of every president of the College of William and Mary save one. Its first occupant, the Reverend James Blair, was the energetic Anglican clergyman who first induced the Virginia Assembly to favor the erection of a college and then, in 1693, persuaded King William and Queen Mary to charter and endow it. He also supervised the con-

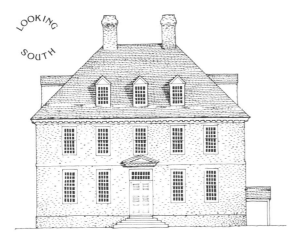

LOOKING SOUTH

* The Brafferton

struction of all the early buildings and selected the first faculty and curriculum. Blair served as president for half a century.

During the last stages of the Revolution, General Cornwallis used the house briefly as his headquarters. French officers serving under General Rochambeau occupied the house for a short time after the siege of Yorktown, causing accidental damage by fire. The French government allocated funds to repair the building.

When Robert Boyle, the noted British scientist, died in 1691, he left his personal property to charitable and pious uses at the discretion of his executors. They invested some of the funds in the manor of Brafferton in Yorkshire. President James Blair persuaded them to give most of the profits from Brafferton to the College of William and Mary to be used for the education and conversion of Indian boys.

At first the Indian students had a classroom in the Wren Building and lodged elsewhere in town. **The Brafferton** was completed for their use in 1723. Until the Revolution cut off revenue from the Boyle foundation, there were always some Indians—often a dozen or more—at the College. Most of them seem to have forgotten their prayers and catechism after they left Williamsburg, however. So far as is known, not one of the Indians became a missionary as Boyle's executors had hoped.

The building suffered remarkably little damage over the years, although Federal troops ripped its interior woodwork from the walls and used it for firewood during the Civil War.

The Brafferton today provides offices.

In the common room the College's valuable "philosophic" apparatus could be kept safely out of students' reach.

Shopping Opportunities

MARY DICKINSON STORE
(Ticket not required)

Goods similar to those sold in the eighteenth century by milliner Mary Dickinson can be purchased in this retail establishment. Straw hats, ribbons, bows, scents, jewelry, silver, caps, and stockings are some of the products available here.

JOHN GREENHOW STORE
(Ticket not required)

A wide variety of items similar to those sold here two hundred years ago is again available in John Greenhow's Store. Fabrics, tinware, baskets, hats, craftsmen's tools and supplies, and many other products are to be found in Mr. Greenhow's store today.

MERCHANTS SQUARE

Almost fifty modern shops and services are available in the Merchants Square area. The ***Williamsburg Theatre*** in Merchants Square presents a current film nightly.

CRAFT HOUSE in Merchants Square offers reproductions of Williamsburg antiques—furniture, glass, silver, brass, pewter, and china. Books, needlework, and many other articles are also available at Craft House. The **Sign of the Rooster,** located downstairs at Craft House, features items reproduced from the Abby Aldrich Rockefeller Folk Art Center collection. The line of folk art products inspired by a variety of decorative and utilitarian objects includes jewelry, toys, furniture, needlework, and accessories for the home. Folk art adaptations such as handcrafted decoys, coverlets, and tinware made especially for Colonial Williamsburg are also sold at the Sign of the Rooster.

American Express, Master-card, and Visa credit cards are accepted at Colonial Williamsburg retail outlets.

Dining Opportunities

A GOOD PLACE TO EAT in Merchants Square serves hot and cold sandwiches, soups, salads, fruits, and beverages. The ice cream counter features distinctive Colonial Williamsburg flavors. The bakery counter offers an assortment of breads, desserts, and pastries from Colonial Williamsburg's bakery.

Other restaurants are available in Merchants Square.

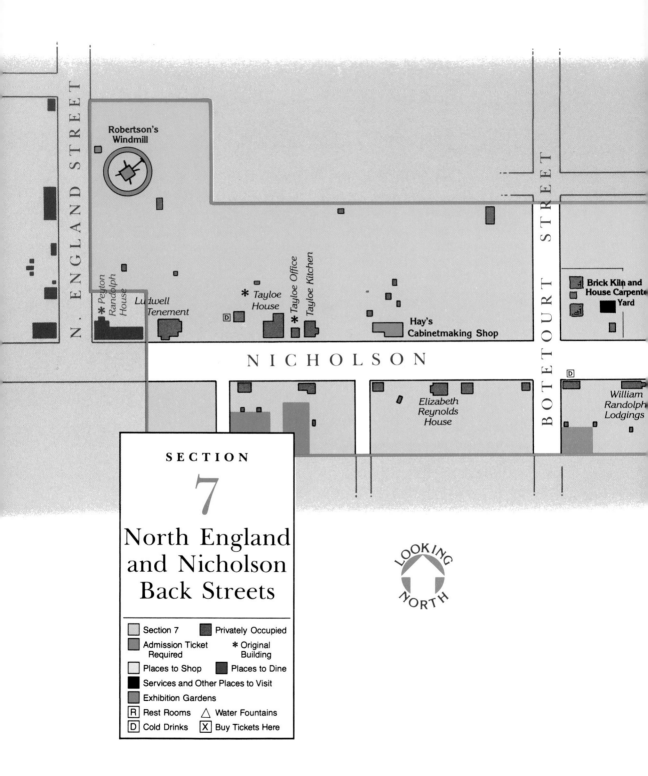

Robertson's Windmill

N. ENGLAND STREET

BOTETOURT STREET

* Peyton Randolph House

Ludwell Tenement

* Tayloe House

* Tayloe Office

Tayloe Kitchen

Hay's Cabinetmaking Shop

Brick Kiln and House Carpente Yard

NICHOLSON

Elizabeth Reynolds House

William Randolph Lodgings

SECTION

7

North England and Nicholson Back Streets

LOOKING NORTH

Section 7

Privately Occupied

Admission Ticket Required

* Original Building

Places to Shop

Places to Dine

Services and Other Places to Visit

Exhibition Gardens

R Rest Rooms

△ Water Fountains

D Cold Drinks

X Buy Tickets Here

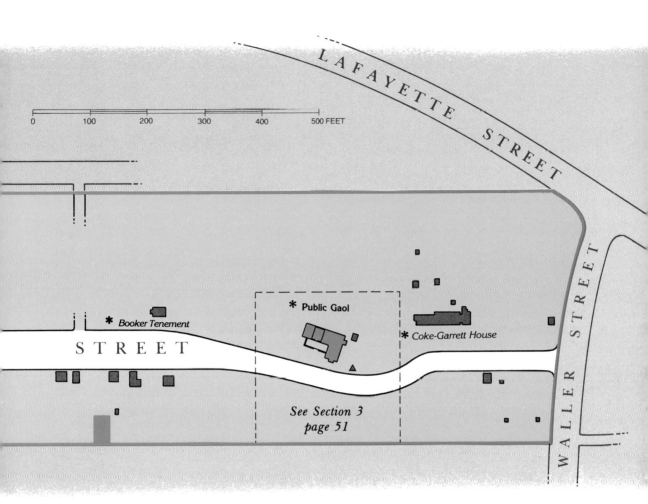

Scale: 0 100 200 300 400 500 FEET

LAFAYETTE STREET

WALLER STREET

* Booker Tenement

STREET

* Public Gaol

* Coke-Garrett House

See Section 3
page 51

North England and Nicholson Back Streets

A mixture of buildings—substantial townhouses and modest dwellings, shops and stores, lodging houses and taverns—characterized North England, Nicholson, Waller, and Francis streets in the eighteenth century. Structures on these back streets were generally spaced farther apart than those along Duke of Gloucester Street. Working sheds, smokehouses, dairies, kitchens (some with attics or lofts for slave quarters), poultry runs, livestock pens, stables, carriage houses, woodpiles, privies—all could be found in the backyards of the colonial capital. This was the workaday world of Williamsburg where slaves and white servants went about the drudgery of everyday life.

Robertson's Windmill has been reconstructed on a site owned in 1723 by William Robertson, clerk of the Council and one of early Williamsburg's leading citizens.

Colonial Virginians depended on the local miller to grind the grain from which they made their bread—a staple of their diet that appeared at nearly every meal. Sometimes colonial householders bought cornmeal or flour for cash, or "ready money." If they brought their own grain to be ground, they might barter with the miller or agree to let him exact his time-honored one-sixth toll.

Two types of windmills existed in the colonial period, the tower mill, a fixed structure of which only the hooded top moved, and the post mill, the earliest form of mill known, which had been used in Europe since the Middle Ages. The post

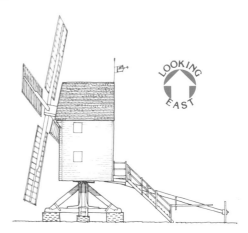

Robertson's Windmill ▉

mill is so called because the whole superstructure revolves on top of a single huge post of hewed timber. The superstructure has two levels. The upper chamber holds

Robertson's Windmill   ▉

Robertson's Windmill is an operating craft where wind-driven stones grind corn and other grains. In colonial days a mill could grind as much as two hundred pounds of cornmeal an hour.

The capriciousness of the wind governed the complex grinding procedure. Without wind, the mill stood idle and the miller earned nothing. When the wind began to blow, whether in the middle of a meal or the middle of the night, the miller had to heed its call to work. And he always had to keep a weather eye on the horizon for signs of too much wind, which could damage the sailcloths.

the main shaft and millstones; the lower chamber holds the screening and sacking machinery. Robertson's Windmill is the post type, which was common in tidewater Virginia in the eighteenth century.

The miller needed an assistant to help keep the mill facing the wind and to manage the grinding and sacking operations. In a high wind the miller had to furl his linen sails, lashing them tightly top and bottom to the lattice frames of the four wide arms of the mill.

An eighteenth-century visitor peering over the fence behind the **Grissell Hay Lodging House** or the **Peyton Randolph House** would have seen servants bustling about cooking and preparing food or stitching, laundering, and drying clothes and household linens. The mistress of the house supervised them. Other slaves tended the garden or worked in the stables located toward the rear of each property.

Archaeologists have located a series of small structures north of the Peyton Ran-

Meet . . . Eve

Eve, one of the slaves in the household of Peyton Randolph, worked in the spinning house in the Randolphs' backyard. In 1776 she had been appraised at one hundred pounds, a sum that indicates she was a skilled adult worker who may have overseen several other slave women and girls.

Spinning appears to have been Eve's main task. The amount of cotton or linen thread or wool yarn she and her fellow slaves were expected to spin each day varied seasonally. So did her workday, which increased from nine or so hours in midwinter to as long as fourteen in midsummer. Eve's mistress, Mrs. Betty Randolph, took the thread and yarn to a local weaver, who wove it into a coarse fabric (often a combination of linen and wool or cotton and wool) that was made into clothing for the Randolphs' slaves.

Despite her skills, Eve found many ways to vex her mistress. Or perhaps it was Mrs. Randolph who proved vexing to Eve. In any case, an annotated draft of an inventory taken on December 20, 1776, named Eve as one of eight Randolph slaves "gone to the enemy." In November 1775 Lord Dunmore promised freedom to any slaves who joined the ranks of his "Ethiopian Regiment" or took up arms against the colonists. Along with hundreds of others, Eve went over to the British. By the summer of 1780, either because she became disillusioned with British promises or because she was recaptured, Eve had returned to Williamsburg.

There was no reconciliation between slave and mistress, however. Although Mrs. Randolph had formerly decided to bequeath Eve and Eve's son George to her niece, Ann Coupland, she changed her mind in a codicil to her will dated July 20, 1782. "Eve's bad behavior laid me under the necessity of selling her," Mrs. Randolph stated flatly, and she directed that part of the money from the sale of Eve be used to buy a young female slave for Miss Coupland.

dolph House near the street line that have been identified as outbuildings. When the property was offered for sale in 1783, an advertisement described it as having "every necessary outhouse convenient for a large family, garden, and yard well paled in," and, along the north side of Scotland Street next to the Palace land, "stables to hold twelve horses and room for two carriages, with several acres of pasture ground."

Randolph's inventory, taken in 1776, suggests that his slaves spun thread and

Ludwell Tenement

Ludwell-Paradise Stable.

yarn and made candles because it lists a parcel of tallow and twenty-three candle molds, five flax wheels, four reels, two spinning wheels, and parcels of wool, hemp, and flax. The inventory also included twenty-seven slaves, as many as one-third of whom may have been hired out to work elsewhere in town, a fairly common practice in the eighteenth century.

In contrast to the relatively flat and straight Duke of Gloucester Street, Nicholson Street is an undulating lane that moves across a series of hills and valleys and crosses several gullies that run from the high ground of the town toward Queen's Creek and eventually to the York River. Geography affected the desirability of lots along Nicholson Street. The high ground was reserved for the few large estates in

* *Tayloe House*   * *Tayloe Office and Kitchen*

the area, leaving the cuts and washes to light industry. For example, the west end of Anthony Hay's cabinetmaking shop is built directly over a stream.

The **Ludwell Tenement,** just to the east of the Peyton Randolph House, reaffirms another characteristic of Williamsburg's back streets: rental property and smaller houses coexisted with the homes of such well-to-do residents as the Randolphs and the Tayloes. In 1770 the Ludwell Tenement was identified as "the Tenement adjoining the Speaker," meaning the rental property next to the home of Peyton Randolph.

Built midway into the eighteenth century, the gambrel-roofed *Tayloe House* changed hands in 1759 for six hundred pounds, a very high price for a frame house at that time. One of the wealthiest men in colonial Virginia, Colonel John Tayloe, owner of the magnificent plantation called Mt. Airy in Richmond County, purchased the building probably for use as a townhouse. Tayloe served on the Council for many years.

The backyard of the Tayloe House extends north from Nicholson Street into what were pastures in colonial times. The remains of an eighteenth-century road leading away from town is still visible next to the Tayloe lot.

The *Tayloe Office* just east of the house has an interesting "ogee," or bell-shaped roof. This too is an original building.

Hay's Cabinetmaking Shop on the north edge of town occupied low ground between two substantial residences. On this site a succession of cabinetmakers made some of the finest furniture in the colonies. Like London and other American cabinetmakers, they also repaired furniture and musical instruments, resilvered mirrors, and made exotic "Gothic" garden

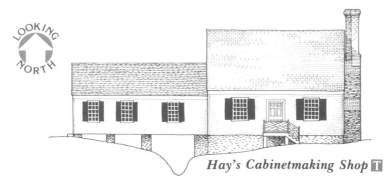

Hay's Cabinetmaking Shop ⊤

fences. Williamsburg cabinetmakers also ran an elaborate funeral service that included expensive coffins and hearse rentals. During the Revolution, workmen in Hay's shop cleaned and repaired arms for the American forces.

Anthony Hay, who had been a cabinetmaker in Williamsburg for several years, bought this lot in 1756. Hay gave up the business in 1766 when he purchased the Raleigh Tavern, but he and his wife continued to live on the property. Subsequent renters of the shop included cabinetmakers Benjamin Bucktrout (who advertised that he also made and repaired spinets and harpsichords) and Edmund Dickinson (probably Hay's former journeyman). Carver and gilder George Hamilton worked here too.

Archaeologists found the waterlogged

⊤

Hay's Cabinetmaking Shop

This reconstructed shop houses a "wareroom," an eighteenth-century term for a combination showroom and warehouse, on the left. Here, away from the noise and dirt of the shop, the cabinetmaker met his customers and conducted the majority of his business. Ready-made furniture available for sale and completed custom pieces awaiting delivery would have been stored in the wareroom.

In the workroom (right), the master, journeymen, and apprentices re-create the working environment of the original shop, using the hand tools and technology of the period to produce furniture and musical instruments, especially harpsichords and spinets. Visitors can learn about the materials, processes, and techniques used in the production of furniture and musical instruments.

Meet . . . Anthony Hay

Anthony Hay, already well established as one of Williamsburg's premier cabinetmakers, bought the property on which his reconstructed shop now stands in 1756. Among the skilled artisans who plied their trade in Hay's shop may be numbered carpenter and joiner Christopher Ford and James Wilson, a carver newly arrived from London.

Hay ceased cabinetmaking late in 1766, purchased the Raleigh Tavern, and turned his woodworking business over to Benjamin Bucktrout. That Hay was wealthy enough to buy the Raleigh Tavern, one of Williamsburg's finest ordinaries, speaks well of his success as a cabinetmaker.

The tradition of superior workmanship which created fine furniture that ranks with the best pieces produced by cabinetmakers in Boston, Philadelphia, or Charleston is the legacy of Anthony Hay and the other master craftsmen who worked in his shop.

Anthony Hay died in 1770, a victim of a painful facial cancer. After enduring several operations on his face and lip, Hay traveled to Prince Edward County where he placed himself under the care of Mrs. Constant Woodson, who claimed that she could cure cancer. Unfortunately, Mrs. Woodson could not help Hay, who died on December 4. Since mahogany dust is a known carcinogen that affects oral and nasal passages, it may be that Hay's disease was the result of an occupational hazard.

---

remains of a fence rail in the stream bed under the western part of the shop. The seven-foot-long artifact showed both the crude form of the wood rail and the spacing between the pickets that had been nailed to it. The fence in front of the shop faithfully reproduces these details. Archaeological discoveries also provided evidence of clay roofing tiles like those that now cover the shop.

Many of the town's smaller households were located on Williamsburg's back streets. The ***Elizabeth Reynolds House*** on the south side of Nicholson Street is one of the few structures on the street that faces north.

In 1777 *Virginia Gazette* printer William

Hunter deeded a narrow strip of land containing a house and garden to his mother, Elizabeth Reynolds. Hunter was illegiti-

Elizabeth Reynolds House

Brick Kiln and House Carpenter's Yard

∗ Booker Tenement

mate, and although his father had acknowledged William in his will, he failed to provide for the boy's mother. Hunter's sense of duty seems to have been greater than his father's. In addition to the house

The master house carpenter at work.

William Randolph Lodgings

and lot, he agreed to pay Elizabeth an annuity of forty pounds and to furnish a "servant maid fit and able to serve wait and attend her."

The **Brick Kiln and House Carpenter's Yard** on the corner of Nicholson and Botetourt streets represent the building trades. The growth of the town in the mid-1700s sustained a concentration of carpenters, bricklayers, plasterers, and glaziers. In the eighteenth century brickmakers usually built a kiln, or "clamp" as they called it, on the site of each large brick house under construction. Carpenters also moved from site to site. Lumber and timber yards were located near the outskirts of town on lots much like this one.

Just down the street is another example of the contrast in land use so commonplace in eighteenth-century Virginia. An unusually narrow building, the **William Randolph Lodgings** was "letten for Lodgins" in 1735 to William Randolph, the uncle of Peyton Randolph. A burgess and later a councillor, William obviously considered this modest structure an appropriate residence when he came to Williamsburg on government business.

The next building on the north side of Nicholson Street, the small one and one-half story **Booker Tenement,** is typical of a Williamsburg house of the "middling sort." An analysis of the tree growth rings in its timbers showed that the wood was cut about 1823. Documentary evidence indicates that Richard Booker, carpenter and town constable, had begun to rent out

* Coke-Garrett House

rooms in his newly built tenement by the spring of 1826.

THE PUBLIC GAOL. A description of the Public Gaol begins on page 60.

Facing south on Nicholson Street near its intersection with Waller Street is the **Coke-Garrett House.** In 1755 John Coke, goldsmith and tavern keeper who already owned a house and three lots immediately to the east, bought the two lots on which the story and one-half west section stands. It dates from the eighteenth century. The one and one half story east section is an eighteenth-century structure that was moved to this site from an unknown location around 1837. The two-story center portion was built about 1836–1837 during the Garrett family's ownership. The brick office that served as Dr. Robert Garrett's surgery after the battle of Williamsburg in 1863 apparently dates from about 1810. Dr. Garrett treated the wounded of both armies here.

The subdued Greek Revival architecture of the center section merges easily with the colonial styles of the east and west wings. The brick office bears full evidence of the Greek Revival style in its columned and pedimented porch. An interesting feature of the eighteenth-century porch on the west wing, one of the few to have survived in tidewater Virginia, is its "Chinese Chippendale" porch railing.

Archaeologists found crucibles with traces of gold and silver, a small silver bar, a gold earring, and an engraver's trial piece—all evidence of John Coke's gold- and silversmithing activities—on the site. They also discovered wine glasses, a fine punch bowl, and other artifacts that could be associated with a tavern.

Coke left a personal estate valued at £772 when he died in 1767. His widow, Sarah, continued to operate or rent out the house as a tavern. Her versatile son, Robey, repaired wagons, mounted cannon, and helved axes during the Revolution. The Garrett family acquired the property in 1810; Garretts owned it for well over a century.

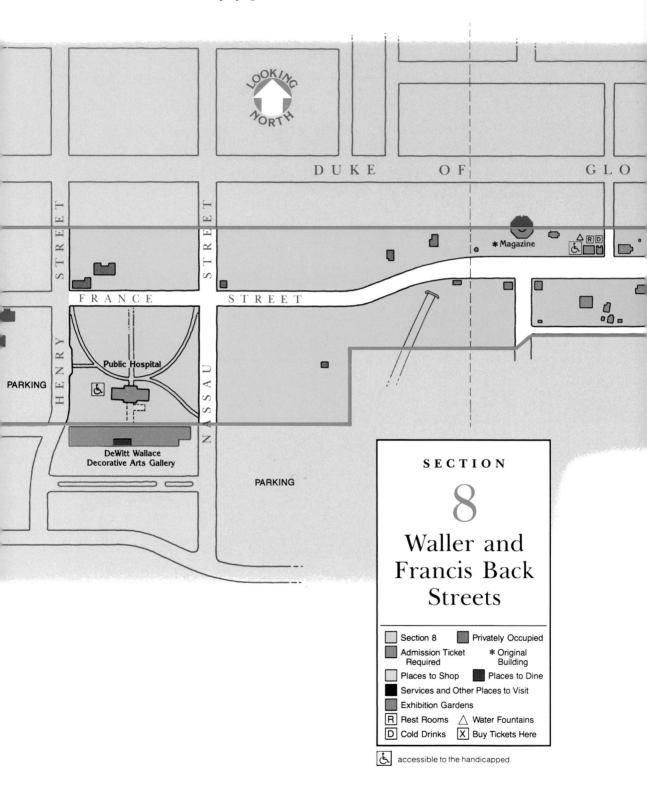

See detailed map, pages 128-129

LOOKING NORTH

D U K E   O F   G L O

S T R E E T (HENRY STREET)

S T R E E T (NASSAU STREET)

F R A N C E   S T R E E T

* Magazine

PARKING

Public Hospital

DeWitt Wallace
Decorative Arts Gallery

PARKING

SECTION

8

Waller and
Francis Back
Streets

Section 8	Privately Occupied
Admission Ticket Required	* Original Building
Places to Shop	Places to Dine
Services and Other Places to Visit	
Exhibition Gardens	
R Rest Rooms	△ Water Fountains
D Cold Drinks	X Buy Tickets Here

♿ accessible to the handicapped.

110

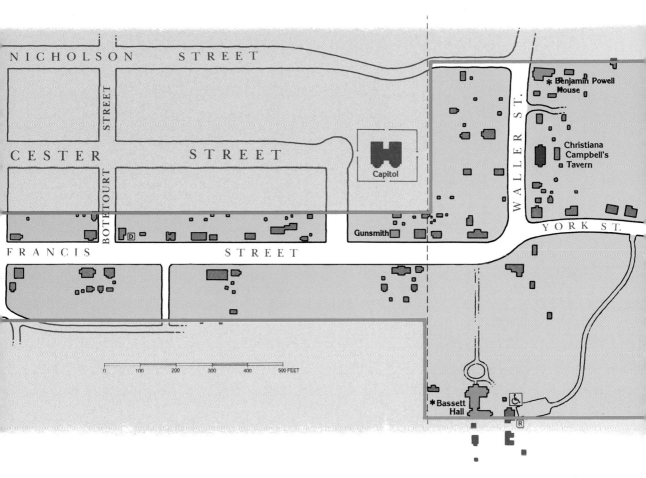

Waller and Francis Back Streets

EARLY in the eighteenth century, Francis and Waller streets defined the southern and eastern limits, respectively, of the colonial capital. Town met country on the south side of Williamsburg. Slave quarters, outbuildings, barns, and fields lay immediately beyond the town's southern boundary. Then the landscape stretched away into broad meadows and wooded hillsides.

The eastern outskirts of town began to change by mid-century. Several recently built lodging houses and taverns catered to transients and townspeople who had business at the nearby Capitol. Williamsburg's second theater became a center of imported British culture, while the racetrack just east of town drew large crowds. As Williamsburg grew, a shortage of residential space in this area spurred the development of subdivisions at the east end of town and along Francis Street. A number of local craftsmen took advantage of the opportunity to buy small lots at attractive prices. Here an artisan could build a dwelling and perhaps open a shop.

111

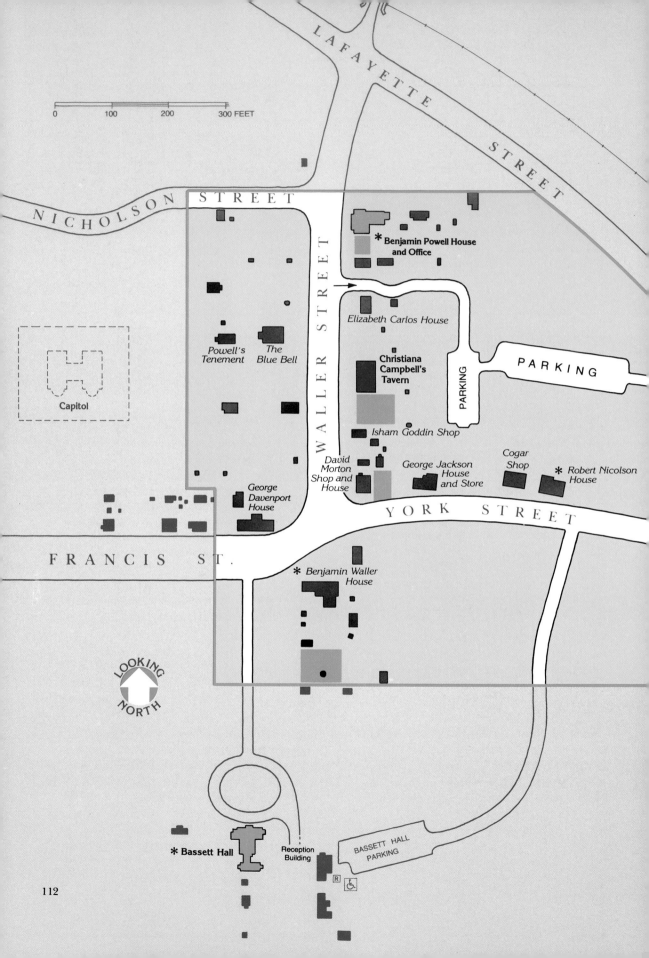

LAFAYETTE STREET

NICHOLSON STREET

0   100   200   300 FEET

Capitol

WALLER STREET

Powell's Tenement

The Blue Bell

* Benjamin Powell House and Office

Elizabeth Carlos House

Christiana Campbell's Tavern

PARKING

PARKING

Isham Goddin Shop

David Morton Shop and House

George Jackson House and Store

Cogar Shop

* Robert Nicolson House

George Davenport House

YORK STREET

FRANCIS ST.

* Benjamin Waller House

LOOKING NORTH

* Bassett Hall

Reception Building

BASSETT HALL PARKING

R

112

* *Benjamin Powell House* 🔳   * *Benjamin Powell Office*   *Elizabeth Carlos House*

The Benjamin Powell House is named for Benjamin Powell, a successful builder who obtained the property in 1763. A general contractor (or "undertaker," to use the eighteenth-century term), Powell worked on a number of public buildings in Williamsburg. He repaired the Public Gaol in 1764 and 1765, built the tower and steeple at Bruton Parish Church in 1769, and put up the Public Hospital between 1771 and 1773. Along with Peyton Randolph, George Wythe, and other men of similar standing, Powell served on a committee that enforced an embargo of selected British goods in 1774.

School groups and the visiting public are accommodated seasonally.

Powell sold the property in 1782 and it changed hands several times before Benjamin Carter Waller, the son of an early owner, bought it in 1794. The small brick building next to the restored house probably served as the office of Waller's son, Dr. Robert Waller, to whom he deeded that part of the property in 1814. The temple-style brick office is similar to the one at the Coke-Garrett House across the street.

Elizabeth Carlos bought the lot on which a story and one-half frame house now stands in 1772. Typical of Williamsburg's more modest dwellings, the dusky brown color of the reconstructed **Elizabeth Carlos House** would have been familiar to early residents since not every house in town was painted white.

A manuscript account book records purchases of gloves, hose, ribbons, thread, and fabric from Mrs. Carlos in 1777 and indicates that she made aprons and gowns. This suggests that Elizabeth Carlos was a milliner and dressmaker who carried on her business in her home.

In 1703 John Redwood, keeper of the Public Gaol, obtained a lot east of the Capitol where he operated an ordinary. At various times in the eighteenth century **The Blue Bell** housed a tavern, a lodging house, a store, a gunsmith's shop, and a tenement. After being informed in 1771 that his Williamsburg property, including The Blue Bell, was in "bad repair always rented to bad tenants, always nasty and few rents paid," absentee owner William Lee of London tried to sell the tavern but failed to find a buyer.

Wheelwright and riding chair maker Peter Powell rented a shop on the site of

    Powell's Tenement   *The Blue Bell*

Christiana Campbell's Tavern   *Isham Goddin Shop*

Powell's Tenement from 1755 to about 1770. In 1756 Powell advertised for an assistant, a blacksmith "who understands doing riding chair work." Later, in 1779, Powell's Tenement was occupied by the keeper of the nearby Public Gaol.

The reconstructed building now houses the heating plant for the Capitol. ***Powell's Kitchen*** is behind.

Christiana Campbell announced in October 1771 that she had recently opened a "Tavern in the House, behind the Capitol" where she promised "genteel Accommodations, and the very best Entertainment," by which she meant food and drink. A distinguished clientele patronized Mrs. Campbell's. When George Washington came to town to attend the House of Burgesses in the spring of 1772, for example, he recorded in his diary that he dined there ten times within two months. Washington and his friends often gathered at ***Christiana Campbell's Tavern*** for refreshments and discussions of everything from horse races to politics.

Today, Mrs. Campbell's brunch, served daily, offers such delicacies as pecan waffles, skillet fried chicken, and a variety of omelets. Dinner features seafood fresh from the Chesapeake Bay.

Isham Goddin, a militiaman from New Kent County, moved to Williamsburg in

Meet . . .
Christiana Campbell

Christiana Campbell, one of Williamsburg's best known tavern keepers, seems to have been born to the trade since her father, John Burdett, ran an ordinary on Duke of Gloucester Street at the Sign of Edinburgh Castle.

When Christiana's husband died at an early age, she turned to tavern keeping as a means of supporting herself and her two young children. From sometime before 1760 until about 1769 the "widow Campbell" kept a tavern on the site of the James Anderson House on Duke of Gloucester Street; in 1771 she moved

David Morton Shop and House

of Masons, served as treasurer of the lodge from 1780 to 1786.

The *George Jackson House and Store* on York Street was once owned by a patriotic merchant who risked his life as well as his fortune during the Revolutionary War.

1778 and acquired the small *Isham Goddin Shop* for two hundred pounds. When he returned to New Kent in 1783, he sold his plot and building for only ninety pounds, a decrease that reflects both wartime inflation and the collapse in the value of real estate in Williamsburg after the capital moved to Richmond.

In 1777 tailor David Morton purchased the lot on the corner of Waller and York streets for four hundred pounds, a sum that indicates the transaction included the *David Morton House and Shop* and the shop next door, which Morton sold to Isham Goddin the next year. Morton, an active member of the Williamsburg Lodge

and briefly operated a tavern at "the Coffee-House in the main street, next to the Capitol"; finally, by early fall of that year, she established her business in the tavern that today bears her name.

Although Christiana gave up tavern keeping about the time the capital moved to Richmond, her establishment's reputation lived on. In 1783 Yorktown merchant Alexander Macaulay thought the tavern was still in operation and ushered his wife into what seems to have been Mrs. Campbell's front parlor. Macaulay demanded that a fire be lit to warm the cold room and ordered "Oysters Cook'd any way." Mrs. Campbell indignantly replied, "I dont keep a house of entertainment, nor have not for some years." Angered by her curt rebuff, Macaulay later retaliated by describing Christiana Campbell as "a little old Woman, about four feet high; and equally thick, a little turn up peg nose, a mouth screw'd up to one side; in short; nothing in any part of her appearance in the least inviting."

George Jackson House and Store

Cogar Shop

Jackson chartered a ship, sailed it to Bermuda, and returned with a supply of much needed gunpowder for the American forces.

Jackson acquired the property shortly after he moved to Williamsburg from Norfolk in 1773 or 1774. The different roof slopes indicate that this building was, in effect, two buildings. The window and door arrangement of the east wing are typical of shops in the eighteenth century, while the rear chimney would have heated a small counting room. Jackson probably used this part of the structure as his store.

The **Cogar Shop,** a small eighteenth-century building, was moved from King and Queen County to this lot in 1947. Colonial Williamsburg later acquired the property.

Robert Nicolson, a tailor and merchant, built the last structure on York Street, the gambrel-roofed **Robert Nicolson House,** about mid-century. The off-center entrance door testifies to two periods of construction, the eastern part possibly as early as 1752 and the western a little later. For several years thereafter Nicolson took in lodgers.

Nicolson initially had his shop across the street. When his eldest son, William, joined him in the tailoring business in 1774, they opened a shop and store on Duke of Gloucester Street, a much better location for commercial purposes. During the Revolution Nicolson served on the local committee of safety. He and William provided uniforms to the American army.

Across the street is the motor vehicle entrance to **Bassett Hall,** the two-story

frame house that served for many years as the Williamsburg home of Mr. and Mrs. John D. Rockefeller, Jr. Bassett Hall is closely associated with the restoration of Williamsburg. Mr. Rockefeller and the Reverend W. A. R. Goodwin, who was instrumental in interesting the philanthropist in restoring Virginia's colonial capital, often met under the three hundred-year-old "Great Oak" in the yard. Abby Aldrich Rockefeller, a founder of the Museum of Modern Art, furnished the house with fine examples of American folk art and created a comfortable family atmosphere conducive to relaxation.

Bassett Hall, its furnishings, and its 585 acres of woodland were bequeathed to Colonial Williamsburg by the Rockefeller family in 1979. The interior of the house is shown substantially as it appeared when Mr. and Mrs. Rockefeller restored and furnished it in the mid-1930s.

The Bassett Hall property is part of a large plot of land that belonged to the Bray family in the seventeenth century.

* *Bassett Hall* T

Robert Nicolson House

Adjacent to the southern town limits of Williamsburg, this tract joined some 950 acres with four lots in the city, a combination that blurred the lines between town and country. In 1753 the acreage and two of the lots passed into the hands of Colonel Philip Johnson, a burgess from King and Queen County, through his wife, Elizabeth Bray. Johnson is believed to have built the original frame dwelling between 1753 and 1766.

Bassett Hall owes its name to Burwell Bassett, who bought the property about 1800 and owned it for nearly forty years. A nephew of Martha Washington, Bassett served as a congressman and a state senator and delegate.

Benjamin Waller acquired the property on which the **Benjamin Waller House** is lo-

* Bassett Hall

Bassett Hall, a two-story eighteenth-century frame house set off by gardens, original outbuildings, and a long, tree-shaded approach, was for many years the Williamsburg home of Mr. and Mrs. John D. Rockefeller, Jr. Bequeathed to the Colonial Williamsburg Foundation in 1979 along with its furnishings and a 585-acre tract of rolling woodland, the house is exhibited much as it was when the Rockefellers furnished and restored it from the mid-1930s onward.

Bassett Hall is one of the museums of Colonial Williamsburg. On display are approximately 125 pieces of American folk art selected by Mrs. Rockefeller, an early enthusiast and collector, that include weather vanes, chalkware, pottery, needlework, and more than seventy pictures.

The Rockefellers enjoyed and preserved the beauty of the native flora and fauna found on the property. Two trails through the Bassett Hall woodland are accessible to visitors who have purchased a ticket.

George Davenport House

cated before 1750, and it remained in the Waller family for over a century. A prominent Williamsburg attorney, Waller was George Wythe's law teacher. He held a variety of offices during an impressive career: burgess, city recorder, judge of the Court of Admiralty, and vestryman of Bruton Parish.

Benjamin Waller probably used the office, which is adjacent to the house on the east, in his law practice. The smokehouse is an original structure. Behind the Benjamin Waller House is a formal garden open to the public. It has been re-created with the help of a sketch drawn in the early 1800s.

Like most old houses, this house is the product of several building phases. The earliest portion is the single large room to the left of the front door. Later on, a center stair passage and then a large formal room for entertaining were added to the west end, followed by a gambrel-roofed extension in the rear.

The horizontal weatherboards, some of them original, on the dormer cheeks are unusual because such boards are generally attached at an angle that matches the roof slope. The ornamental fence pickets at the east end of the yard are copied from a surviving eighteenth-century specimen that had been used in reroofing the house during the nineteenth century.

The *George Davenport House* across the street once belonged to attorney George Davenport, whose descendants owned the property until 1779. In 1780 John Draper, a blacksmith who had come to Virginia with Governor Botetourt in 1768, bought the property. Draper operated a blacksmith and farrier business on Duke of Gloucester Street.

In 1765 seventeen local residents received permission from the York County Court "for occasional Worship" at a house "situate on a part of a Lott belonging to Mr. George Davenport as a place for Public Worship of God according to the Practice of Protestant Dissenters of the Presbyterian denomination."

* *Benjamin Waller House*

Meet . . .
Benjamin Waller

During his busy and long lifetime (1716–1786), Benjamin Waller became a respected and influential lawyer, civil servant, community leader, and land developer. He studied at the College of William and Mary and then became a clerk in the office of the secretary of the colony, John Carter. Later he practiced law and imparted some of his legal training to George Wythe.

Due in part to the influence of his patron, Secretary Carter, Waller received appointments to a number of important and lucrative positions. He served as clerk and burgess for James City County, recorder of Williamsburg, vestryman of Bruton Parish Church, and judge of the Court of Admiralty, to name a few of his many offices.

Waller purchased several parcels of land on the east side of Williamsburg and subdivided a portion of the property into smaller lots, many of which were bought by craftsmen who paid ten pounds for each lot. Purchasers had to agree to build a sixteen by twenty-foot house with a brick chimney within three years.

Benjamin Waller's grandson, William, subsequently owned and occupied the house with his wife, Elizabeth, the daughter of President John Tyler.

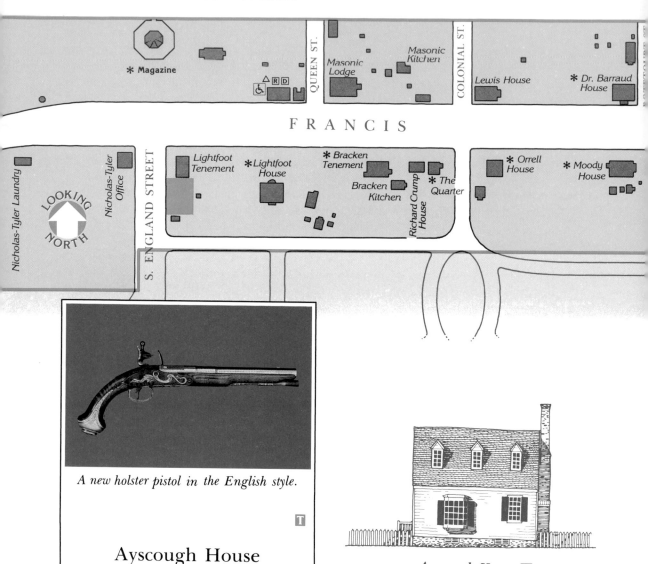

A new holster pistol in the English style.

Ⓣ

Ayscough House

(Gunsmith)

Gunsmithing is a complex trade. The men who master it must fashion iron, steel, brass, silver, and wood to produce firearms that are both functional and pleasing to the eye. Today's gunsmiths use the tools and methods of their predecessors to make rifles, fowling pieces, and pistols like those made in colonial Virginia.

Ayscough House Ⓣ

The ***James Moir House*** and ***James Moir Shop*** are named for James Moir, who owned this property from 1777 to about 1800 and operated his tailoring business on the site.

Walker Maury, a 1775 graduate of the College of William and Mary, established a grammar school in the old Capitol in 1784. In an effort to supplement his income, Moir advertised that he had "furnished his house to accommodate eight or ten [pupils] with the greatest degree of conve-

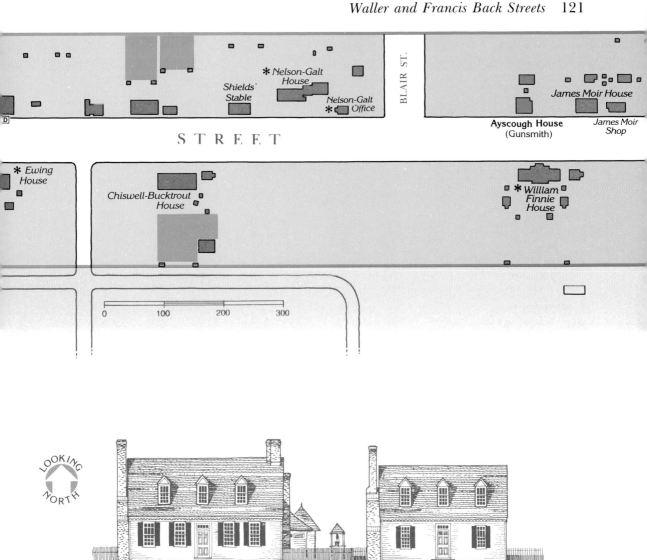

James Moir House

James Moir Shop

niency." Moir offered "to lodge, board, wash and mend for them, at a very low price."

Christopher Ayscough, a former gardener, and his wife, Anne, who had been the head cook for Lieutenant Governor Fauquier at the Palace, purchased the **Ayscough House** and established a tavern there in 1768. The funds probably came from a bequest of two hundred fifty pounds that Governor Fauquier left his cook "in recompense of her great fidelity and attention to me in all my illnesses and of the great Economy with which she conducted the Expenses of my Kitchen during my residence at Williamsburg."

The Ayscoughs' tavern keeping venture proved to be short-lived, however. Within two years Christopher Ayscough, deeply in debt, offered to sell his dwelling along with furnishings, Madeira wine, slaves, and horses. Ayscough then became the doorkeeper at the Capitol, but in 1771 he was discharged for drunkenness.

Shields' Stable

* *Nelson-Galt House*

In a letter written in 1809, St. George Tucker called the **William Finnie House** on the south side of Francis Street "the handsomest house in town." It is a precursor of the classicism that began to change the American architectural scene after the Revolution.

From the 1770s to the mid-1780s, William Finnie and his family lived here. During the American Revolution, Finnie served as quartermaster general of the Southern Department.

James Semple, judge, and professor of law at the College, acquired the property in 1800 and insured the house and all of its outbuildings for two thousand dollars. A sketch of the front of the house drawn on the insurance declaration documents that the house looked then just as it does today. The William Finnie House is depicted on the Frenchman's Map of 1782. The small building just east of the William Finnie House is also an original structure.

In the eighteenth century several lots—now vacant—along Francis Street combined with property south of the town's boundary to form urban estates. People who lived here often described their residences as being "pleasantly situated."

The **Nelson-Galt House** on the north side of Francis Street is one of the oldest buildings on the street. William Robertson, clerk of the Council, bought the property and built a house on it early in the eighteenth century.

Thomas Nelson, a member of a prominent Yorktown family, owned the house later in the century. General Nelson, who signed the Declaration of Independence, commanded Virginia's forces during the Yorktown campaign and succeeded Thomas Jefferson as the third governor of the Commonwealth of Virginia.

Dr. Alexander Dickie Galt, visiting physician at the Public Hospital, purchased the house in 1823. Descendants of the Galt

* **William Finnie Quarters**

* **William Finnie House**

Nelson-Galt Kitchen and Office ✱

established the original form of the roof.

In 1766 Colonel John Chiswell became the center of a scandal that "put the whole country into a ferment." Arrested for killing Robert Rutledge in a fit of rage during a tavern brawl, Colonel Chiswell was arrested for murder. As was customary in such cases, bail was refused, but three of the colonel's friends, who were also judges of the General Court, reversed the decision and Chiswell was released on bail. The less privileged attributed this unusually lenient procedure to the colonel's political and family connections. The colonel died just before his trial—by his own hand, it was rumored.

Cabinetmaker Benjamin Bucktrout resided and worked here by the 1770s.

The *Ewing House* derived its name from Ebenezer Ewing, a Scotch merchant. When he died in 1795, Ewing left the house to Elizabeth Ashton, the mother of his illegitimate son Thomas, with the proviso that "the moment she marries . . . it becomes the property of my son." Elizabeth remained single until her death four years later when young Thomas inherited the house. In 1805 the Williamsburg Hustings Court ordered the legal guardian "to bond out Thomas Ewing for three years to learn the art of seaman or mariner"; Thomas disappeared before completing his apprenticeship.

Josias Moody, a blacksmith, owned the unpretentious house next door from 1794 until he died about 1810. Architectural evidence suggests that the *Moody House*

family, residents of Williamsburg since colonial days, continued to live here until recently.

The small office close to the front of the lot is also original. In the eighteenth century, the word "office" described any outbuilding not otherwise designated as to use.

The next structure to the west on Francis Street is an unpainted stable that is located at the back of the lot belonging to Shields' Tavern, which fronts on Duke of Gloucester Street. The rough appearance of *Shields' Stable* is probably typical of many backyard outbuildings in colonial Williamsburg.

The elongated hipped-roof line of the *Chiswell-Bucktrout House* is a style unusual in Williamsburg although it was common in England at the beginning of the eighteenth century. A study of roof timbers and numbered beams in the surviving portions of the largely reconstructed dwelling

Chiswell-Bucktrout House

LOOKING SOUTH

✱ *Ewing House*

dates from the second quarter of the eighteenth century. The house was altered several times before reaching its present size and appearance by 1782. The long lean-to roof on the back of the Moody House indicates that additions were made to an earlier structure.

The **Dr. Barraud House** on the northwest corner of Francis and Botetourt streets was erected before 1782 and incorporated earlier buildings on the site. Dr. Philip Barraud, the buyer in 1783, was born in Virginia, saw active service during the Revolution, studied medicine at the University of Edinburgh, and, with Dr.

Lewis House

John Minson Galt, served as visiting physician to the Public Hospital until he moved to Norfolk in 1799.

The Dr. Barraud House is one of the few residences that front Francis Street on the north. For the most part, the north side of Francis Street gives access to the back of Duke of Gloucester Street lots. This is where stables and privies were usually located in the eighteenth century.

The **Lewis House** is named for Charles Lewis, who owned the property until 1806 and is believed to have built the original house. Initially the lot was part of the Or-

* *Moody House*

Meet . . . Adam Waterford

Blacks made up about half of the population of Williamsburg before the Revolution. Most of them were slaves; most performed domestic duties; nearly all were illiterate. Furthermore, no slave was permitted to own property. Adam Waterford, a free black who made his living as a cooper, was therefore unusual: he was free; he had learned a trade; he had acquired basic reading and writing skills; and he owned a piece of land.

Coopering was much in demand in tidewater Virginia in the eighteenth century. People used casks—firkins, hogsheads, rundlets, and tuns, to name just a few of the different sizes and shapes of barrels—to transport all sorts of goods. Waterford had managed to clear enough profit from his trade to buy a lot, on which he paid taxes, behind the Chiswell-Bucktrout House.

Although Waterford was free, his wife, Rachel, was not. She belonged to tavern keeper Gabriel Maupin, for whom she worked as a chambermaid and laundress. Adam realized that it would take years to accumulate enough money to buy Rachel's freedom—if Maupin agreed to sell her. In the meantime, any children born to Adam and Rachel while Rachel was still a slave were the property of Maupin.

* Dr. Barraud House

Bracken Tenement to the west and the **Bracken Kitchen,** which is located between the two dwellings.

The popular clergyman's rise to social and financial prominence began in 1776 when he married Sally Burwell of Carter's Grove plantation. He was the rector of Bruton Parish Church for forty-five years, mayor of Williamsburg in 1796, and president of the College of William and Mary from 1812 to 1814.

As the rector grew older, he grew rotund and perhaps overfond of the grape. In 1815 one observer recounted how he

lando Jones property, which extended from Duke of Gloucester Street to Francis Street.

Probably built during the third quarter of the eighteenth century, the **Orrell House** takes its name from John Orrell, who acquired the property about 1810.

The entrance hall, or "passage," of the house, an otherwise typical gambrel-roofed house, is not centered, so all of the living quarters are to one side of the passage. The house forms on plan an exact square whose sides measure twenty-eight feet, and because the roof ridge is twenty-eight feet above the top of the basement wall, it is proportioned as an ideal geometric cube.

Little is known about **The Quarter,** a small nineteenth-century cottage, although it is believed that it served for a time as slave quarters. The addition of a shed portion at the rear has resulted in an unusual and attractive roof line.

The **Richard Crump House** is named for its late eighteenth-century owner. The Reverend Mr. John Bracken, who had extensive real estate holdings along Francis Street, owned it briefly along with the

* Orrell House

kept a couple waiting at the altar. Apparently the "Round Bellied Vicar" imbibed a drop too much on his way to Yorktown to conduct the wedding. He lost his way, "upset the jigg and broke it," and arrived—wet and muddy—an hour late for the ceremony.

The one and one-half story Bracken Tenement has a steep A-shaped gable roof and massive T-shaped chimneys, characteristics of early eighteenth-century architecture in Virginia.

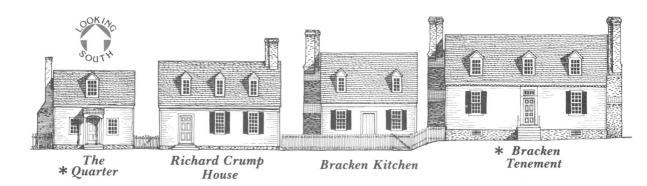

* The
* Quarter

Richard Crump
House

Bracken Kitchen

* Bracken
Tenement

Masonic Lodge   *Masonic Kitchen*

The ***Masonic Kitchen*** and ***Masonic Lodge*** on the north side of Francis Street stand where "the ancient and loyal society of free and accepted Masons" met in the late eighteenth century. Although not chartered until 1773, the Williamsburg chapter had been meeting at local taverns since mid-century. Its members included Peyton Randolph, Peter Pelham, Bishop James Madison, St. George Tucker, and James Monroe.

In the 1770s the lodge held its regular meetings at Market Square Tavern, while they patronized Christiana Campbell's for balls and special entertainments. The Masons leased a portion of this lot and met in a building on this property from the 1780s onward.

Architectural evidence suggests that the ***Lightfoot House,*** built about 1730, was brought to its final form in the 1750s. This fine brick residence is unusual in having a second floor as high as the first. It is adorned by a string course in molded brick and by a wrought-iron balcony suggestive of the one at the Palace. The decorative front fence shows the Chinese, or "chinoiserie," influence so popular about 1750.

The Lightfoot family owned this property during much of the eighteenth century. In 1783 Philip Lightfoot advertised the house for sale, describing it as "a large two story brick dwelling house, with four rooms on a floor; its situation is esteemed one of the most pleasant in the City, lying on the back-street near the market." The Reverend John Bracken, who owned other lots along Francis Street, bought the property in 1786.

The Lightfoot House has been furnished with fine antiques and is equipped with modern conveniences in order to serve as an appropriate guesthouse for distinguished visitors to Williamsburg.

The Reverend Bracken also bought the

*   Lightfoot House*   *Lightfoot Tenement*

The handsome brick Lightfoot House provides comfortable accommodations for VIP visitors to Williamsburg. The style of the "Chinese Chippendale" front fence was fashionable about 1750.

Lightfoot Tenement next door. In the eighteenth century the term "tenement" meant simply a rented house. The garden behind the Lightfoot Tenement is open to the public.

All that remains on the site of the **Nicholas-Tyler House** on the southwest corner of South England Street are two buildings. The **Nicholas-Tyler Office** and **Nicholas-Tyler Laundry** have been reconstructed on their original foundations.

Robert Carter Nicholas bought the property in 1770 and built a large frame house with numerous outbuildings. Nicholas served as treasurer of the colony of Virginia and later as a judge of the Chancery Court.

Among the subsequent owners was John Tyler, tenth president of the United States. Tyler and his family were living here when two horsemen reined up in front of the house early on the morning of April 5, 1841. They knocked on the door and waited. John Tyler, clad in a nightshirt and cap, finally opened the door, only to learn that President William Henry Harrison had died and the awesome duties of the presidency now rested on his shoulders.

Nicholas-Tyler Office

Nicholas-Tyler Laundry

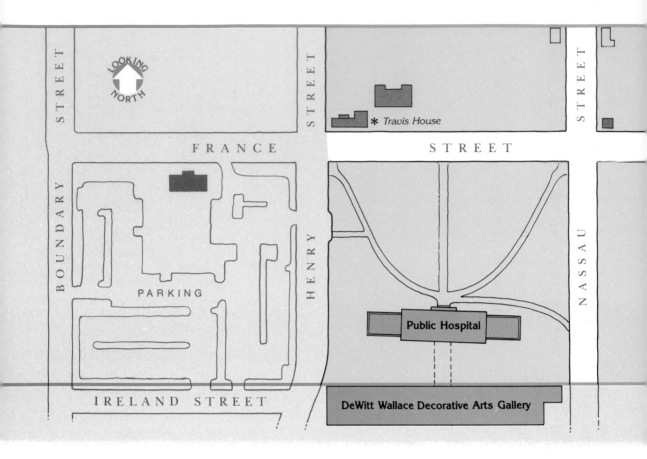

Travis House

FRANCE STREET

STREET

BOUNDARY STREET

PARKING

HENRY

IRELAND STREET

Public Hospital

NASSAU STREET

DeWitt Wallace Decorative Arts Gallery

LOOKING NORTH

Francis Street Becomes France Street

In the eighteenth century the steep sides and muddy bottom of the ravine just ahead separated Francis Street on the east from France Street. Today they form a thoroughfare, with only a dip and curve to mark the end of one and the beginning of the other.

Standing alone on the south side of the street is the **Custis Kitchen.** It marks the

LOOKING SOUTH

* *Custis Kitchen*

eight lots owned by Colonel John Custis—scholar, planter, and eccentric—who settled in Williamsburg about 1715.

Here Custis built a substantial brick house and a number of outbuildings and cultivated his celebrated garden, one of the most ambitious ornamental and experimental gardens in early America. Correspondence that records Custis's exchange of plant specimens with the great English natural history enthusiast, Peter Collinson, has been helpful in planting the gardens of Williamsburg.

When Custis died in 1749 his son, Daniel Parke Custis, inherited Custis Square. Daniel's widow, Martha, subsequently married George Washington, who administered the property until his stepson, John Parke ("Jacky") Custis, came of age in 1778.

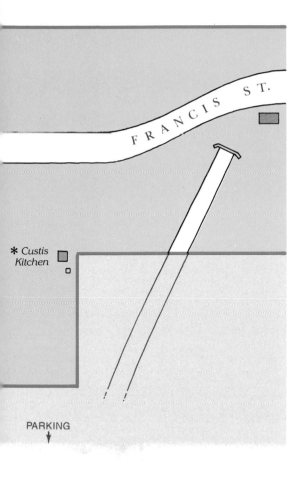

with other dependent people—beggars, vagrants, the elderly, the handicapped— and were dealt with by local officials in a haphazard and unsystematic fashion. Some were even confined to the Public Gaol in Williamsburg.

The General Assembly enacted legislation "to make Provision for the support and maintenance of idiots, lunatics, and other persons of unsound Minds" in 1770. The first public institution in British North America devoted exclusively to the care and treatment of the mentally ill opened in 1773. Robert Smith, a well known Philadelphia architect, designed the building. George Wythe, John Blair, and Thomas Nelson were among its original trustees.

The Public Hospital continued to minister to the mentally ill of the Commonwealth of Virginia until a disastrous fire that destroyed the colonial building swept the facility in 1885. The hospital was rebuilt on this site, where it remained until Eastern State Hospital on the outskirts of Williamsburg opened in the mid-1960s.

The reconstructed Public Hospital follows the form and details of the original building, which have been determined by archaeological investigations and historical research. Exhibits show how the treatment of mental illness evolved. An underground concourse connects the hospital with the contemporary, two-level DeWitt Wallace Decorative Arts Gallery.

Francis Fauquier, one of the colony's most popular royal governors, first proposed the establishment of the **Public Hospital** to the House of Burgesses in 1766. Until that time the insane in Virginia were usually lumped

Public Hospital

LOOKING NORTH

✳ *Travis House*

DEWITT WALLACE DECORATIVE ARTS GALLERY. A description of the DeWitt Wallace Decorative Arts Gallery begins on page 135. The Gallery is entered through the Public Hospital.

On the north side of France Street is the ***Travis House,*** a long gambrel-roofed frame structure. Colonel Edward Champion Travis, a member of the House of Burgesses, erected the western portion of this dwelling before 1765; later residents added on to the house over the next half-century until it reached its present seventy-foot length. The additions are marked today by the vertical boards that originally were the corner boards of their respective sections. The superintendents of the Public Hospital lived in the Travis House until early in this century.

Public Hospital

The first public institution in British North America devoted exclusively to the care and treatment of the mentally ill opened in 1773. It continued to minister to those with mental illness until a fire in 1885 destroyed all of the colonial buildings.

The Public Hospital is the last major public building of eighteenth-century Williamsburg to have been reconstructed. A re-created late eighteenth-century cell has a pallet on the floor, chains on the wall, and bars at the window. The treatment of the mentally ill became more humane in the nineteenth century, a development that is reflected in a re-created mid-nineteenth-century apartment, which is more comfortably furnished.

An interpretive exhibit graphically traces the different theories about mental illness and the methods of treating it that were in fashion between 1773 and 1885. An audiovisual program presents a brief history of the Public Hospital.

The DeWitt Wallace Decorative Arts Gallery is entered through the lower lobby of the Public Hospital.

Dining Opportunities

CHRISTIANA CAMPBELL'S TAVERN

(ticket not required)

The gracious experience of dining in the atmosphere of two hundred years ago awaits those who patronize Christiana Campbell's Tavern. Seafood from the Chesapeake Bay is featured and traditional Virginia and southern foods—fried chicken, spoon bread, and Virginia ham—are offered at brunch and dinner.

American Express, Mastercard, and Visa credit cards are accepted.

Seafood fresh from the Chesapeake Bay is a specialty at Christiana Campbell's Tavern, once run by one of Williamsburg's most renowned hostesses.

The Public Hospital and entrance to the DeWitt Wallace Decorative Arts Gallery.

132

THE MUSEUMS

Public Hospital ^T

*"Every civilized Country has an Hospital for these
People, where they are confined, maintained and attended by able Physicians, to endeavour to restore to
them their lost reason."*

GOVERNOR Francis Fauquier presented this rationale in 1766 when
he first proposed that a hospital be
founded to care "for these miserable Objects, who cannot help themselves." On
June 4, 1770, the House of Burgesses
passed a bill to establish the Public Hospital, which opened in the fall of 1773 as the
first public institution in the British North
American colonies devoted solely to the
care and treatment of the mentally ill.

Over the next eleven decades the Public
Hospital grew into a complex of nine
buildings. As the physical appearance of
the hospital changed, so too did the ways
in which mental illness was regarded and
treated.

During the period 1773–1835, the hospital was part prison, part infirmary. Its
first keeper, James Galt, had formerly
been in charge of the Public Gaol. His wife,
Mary, became the matron for the female
patients. Dr. John de Sequeyra, a physician
educated in Holland, served as the attending doctor from 1773 to 1795. He saw patients when they were admitted and once a
week thereafter. A court of directors
drawn from Virginia's gentry class determined admissions, ordered discharges,
and made policy decisions. Only those persons considered dangerous or curable
were admitted.

Physicians in this "Age of Restraint" regarded mental illness as a disease of the
brain, and the belief that mentally disturbed persons could be cured by using
scientific knowledge was relatively new. To
calm or cure patients, the staff applied
mechanical restraints, prescribed potent
drugs, employed the ducking chair or
plunge bath, and used bleeding instruments.

*The interior of a patient's room or cell as it would
have appeared in the Public Hospital during the
late eighteenth century.*

The "Moral Management Era," 1836–
1862, saw a new approach to mental health
care. Moral management deemphasized
restraints and stressed the importance of
kindness in efforts to cure the mentally ill.
Physical labor, organized leisure time ac-

tivities, and careful medical supervision were also important aspects of everyday life in the Public Hospital during this period. Patients were urged to participate in crafts, gardening, and musical diversions and to talk with one another and with the staff.

The hospital's physical facilities and patient population grew dramatically by the mid-nineteenth century. A third floor was added to the original structure and other buildings were enlarged. By 1859 the hospital housed three hundred patients in seven buildings.

Although the hospital had grown in size by the late nineteenth century, the per-

The interior of a patient's apartment as it would have appeared at the Williamsburg asylum during the mid-1840s.

centage of patients successfully treated declined drastically. The staff lost confidence in their ability to cure mental illness, and, without a clear sense of direction, the facility became a long-term home for the chronically ill. The Public Hospital had entered its third phase, the "Custodial Care Regime," 1862–1885.

Physical restraints reappeared and a maintenance program of passive diversions such as magic lantern shows, fishing excursions, picnics, and tea parties was instituted. The number of patients rose to over 440 by 1883 and it became clear that the authorities had decided simply to care

for the mentally disturbed without initiating a course of treatment that might result in a cure.

On the night of June 7, 1885, a fire of undetermined origin completely destroyed the eighteenth-century Public Hospital building, which was reconstructed by the Colonial Williamsburg Foundation in 1985.

The interpretive exhibit in the east wing of the reconstructed Public Hospital has two parts. From the central hall visitors enter the east passage, a reconstructed historic space that contained six cells (of the total of twenty-four) found in the original building. On the north side of the passage is a central viewing room. From this modern vantage point visitors can look into a re-created eighteenth-century cell, a cold and spare prison-like interior with chains on the wall and bars at the window. Opposite is a mid-nineteenth-century apartment, a more comfortable environment in which patients were encouraged to communicate with other patients and with the staff. The exhibition cells contrast the treatments and doctor-patient relationships followed in the eighteenth century with those that became popular in the nineteenth century.

Visitors then cross the passage and enter the exhibition area on the south side of the building. This modern space contains a three-part exhibit that graphically shows the different theories about mental illness and methods of treating it that were in fashion from the opening of the Public Hospital until the devastating fire in 1885. An audiovisual program presents a brief history of the hospital.

The completion of the Public Hospital, eighteenth-century Williamsburg's last major public building to be reconstructed, adds an important dimension to the presentation and interpretation of everyday life in Virginia's colonial capital.

DeWitt Wallace Decorative Arts Gallery ▣

Porcelain drummer boy and stand.

THE DeWitt Wallace Decorative Arts Gallery is a bi-level contemporary museum contained within a high brick wall immediately behind the reconstructed Public Hospital. The gallery is entered through the hospital lobby at the lower level. Completed in 1985 with funds provided by the late DeWitt Wallace, founder of *Reader's Digest,* the museum contains 62,000 square feet, 26,000 of which is devoted to the exhibition and interpretation of a broad range of primarily English and American decorative arts. Dating from the seventeenth century to the early nineteenth century, these examples include furniture, ceramics, silver and base metals, paintings, prints, textiles and costumes, and many other domestic objects from the Colonial Williamsburg collections.

Designed by the internationally honored architect Kevin Roche, the museum is contemporary in concept and offers versatility in both function and presentation. The main floor is penetrated by two symmetrically positioned glass roofed garden courts that allow controlled sunlight to illuminate the adjacent galleries. A handsome stairway draws visitors through the lower level Introductory Gallery and leads them up to the main, or ground, level where the primary exhibition areas are located.

Three types of gallery spaces occupy the main level: selected masterworks, individual media study galleries, and galleries for special exhibitions. Encircling the balcony overlooking the garden court is the Selected Masterworks Gallery featuring objects of great rarity, aesthetic distinction, and technological virtuosity. Arranged in a

The superb tall case clock has works by Thomas Tompion.

Philadelphia chest on chest.

GEORGE WASHINGTON by Charles Willson Peale.

Richmond Cup.

chronological sequence of mixed media, this selection includes English objects such as a magnificent tall case clock made by Thomas Tompion of London for King William III and an extraordinary two-handled silver-gilt urn presented as a racing cup. American objects shown here include Charles Willson Peale's well-known portrait of George Washington, the stately Williamsburg-made governor's chair for the Capitol, and a finely detailed mahogany Philadelphia chest-on-chest.

Exhibition space on either side of the Selected Masterworks Gallery is devoted to a series of study galleries organized by media where English and American textiles, prints, metals, and ceramics are permanently displayed. Furniture is exhibited in the Elizabeth Ridgeley and Miodrag Blagojevich Furniture Gallery. In these more intimate spaces, museum visitors can quietly study and absorb subtle differences in style and technique as they view greater quantities of objects that span a broader range of aesthetic and technical accomplishment.

The remaining third of the museum's exhibition area, located at the east end of the main level and surrounding a restful skylit court, is devoted to special exhibitions drawn from Colonial Williamsburg's holdings and from other sources.

In a wide variety of ways, the objects in these galleries—some of which probably might not have come to Williamsburg because of a variety of factors—help visitors better understand how colonial Virginians, many of whom were transplanted Englishmen or their descendants, became Americans. Introductory tours of the Decorative Arts Gallery are offered daily to complement and enhance visitors' experiences in the Historic Area.

Special lectures, musical events, craft programs, and video presentations are offered (according to a published schedule) in a 240-seat auditorium named for June S. and Joseph H. Hennage. Decorative arts publications as well as reproductions of some of the objects exhibited in the gallery may be purchased in the museum shop adjoining the lower lobby. Luncheon, tea, and other light refreshments are available in the gallery's cafe on the lower level beside the central court.

Two magnificent bed counterpanes, a pair of ornately fashioned silver gilt baskets, and an English mahogany settee are featured in the Selected Masterworks Gallery.

Coffeepot and cracker or bun tray.

Peaceable Kingdom of the Branch by Edward Hicks.

Mrs. Seth Wilkinson by an unidentified artist.

Album quilt made about 1850 by Sarah Anne Whittington Lankford and others.

Abby Aldrich Rockefeller Folk Art Center ▪

AMERICAN folk art is the product of talented but minimally trained or untrained artists and craftspeople working outside the mainstream of academic art. Since colonial times, America's untutored artists have recorded aspects of everyday life, making novel and effective use of whatever media were at hand. Bold colors, simplified shapes, imaginative surface patterns, and the artist's highly original and unself-conscious use of various media are characteristics of the best objects created by amateurs and artisans.

Among the objects on view at the Abby Aldrich Rockefeller Folk Art Center are pictures done in oil, watercolor, ink, and needlework that describe a variety of subjects such as portraits, land- and seascapes, scenes of daily life, biblical, historical, and literary pieces, still lifes, fraktur, and family records. Three-dimensional carvings or sculpture executed in wood and metal include weather vanes and wind toys, ship carvings, shop signs, toys, and decoys. Among household furnishings are boxes, woven and quilted bed coverings, pottery, tinware, iron and steel utensils, and furniture embellished with painted decoration. Objects date from colonial times to the present.

Abby Aldrich Rockefeller pioneered in collecting American folk art in the late 1920s at a time when others ignored its aesthetic appeal and often considered the material curious, quaint, or worth saving only because of its historical associations. Mrs. Rockefeller sought out and acquired over four hundred pieces of folk art in a ten-year period. In 1935 she loaned the principal part of her collection to Colonial Williamsburg, and in 1939 the loan became a gift. Her collection is now housed in a museum, built in her memory by her husband, John D. Rockefeller, Jr., which opened in 1957. The present collection numbers more than two thousand objects and continues to grow through gifts and purchases. The Center offers changing exhibitions of American folk art from its permanent holdings and sponsors major loan shows on a regular basis. The Folk Art Center also houses and maintains extensive research materials on its subject.

Approximately 125 pieces of American folk art selected by Mrs. Rockefeller are on display at Bassett Hall, for many years the Williamsburg home of Mr. and Mrs. John D. Rockefeller, Jr. See pages 116–117.

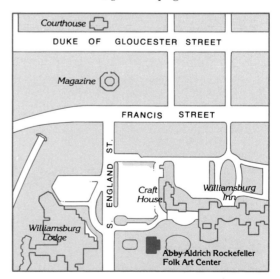

THE COUNTRY ROAD links Williamsburg with Carter's Grove plantation. Reminiscent of the approach to many riverside plantations in the eighteenth century, the Country Road winds through woodlands and traverses marshes and tidal creeks. It terminates at the visitor reception center near the mansion.

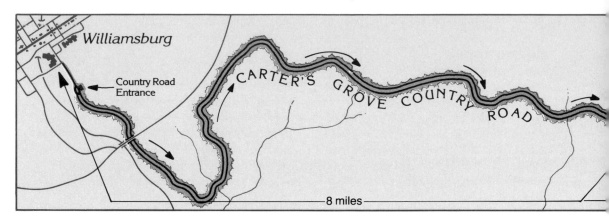

Carter's Grove ▧

ON December 12, 1751, Carter Burwell brought his horse to a stop and dismounted in front of the *Virginia Gazette* printing office on Duke of Gloucester Street. Burwell (pronounced "Burl") had ridden to Williamsburg from Carter's Grove, his plantation on the James River eight miles southeast of the colonial capital. He wanted to purchase a copy of *Palladio Londinensis, or the London Art of Building* by William Salmon, published initially in England in 1734. There were subsequent editions; Burwell probably bought a book printed in 1748.

Burwell was in the process of building a handsome Georgian mansion at Carter's Grove, so he was anxious to obtain Salmon's book. He probably consulted other English handbooks during the planning and initial stages of construction. Nothing in the surviving documentary records or

account books, however, indicates that anyone other than Carter Burwell and the expert craftsmen he hired served as an architect for Carter's Grove.

The mansion that Carter Burwell built stands on part of a 1,400-acre tract purchased early in the eighteenth century by his maternal grandfather, Robert "King" Carter, the progenitor of a large, wealthy, and influential clan in Virginia. When he died in 1732, Carter was reputed to have owned three hundred thousand acres of land, one thousand slaves, and ten thousand pounds sterling.

"King" Carter bought Carter's Grove plantation for the benefit of his eldest daughter, Elizabeth, during her lifetime and afterward for the inheritance of her second son, Carter Burwell. In his will the princely Carter proclaimed that henceforth the estate should "in all times to

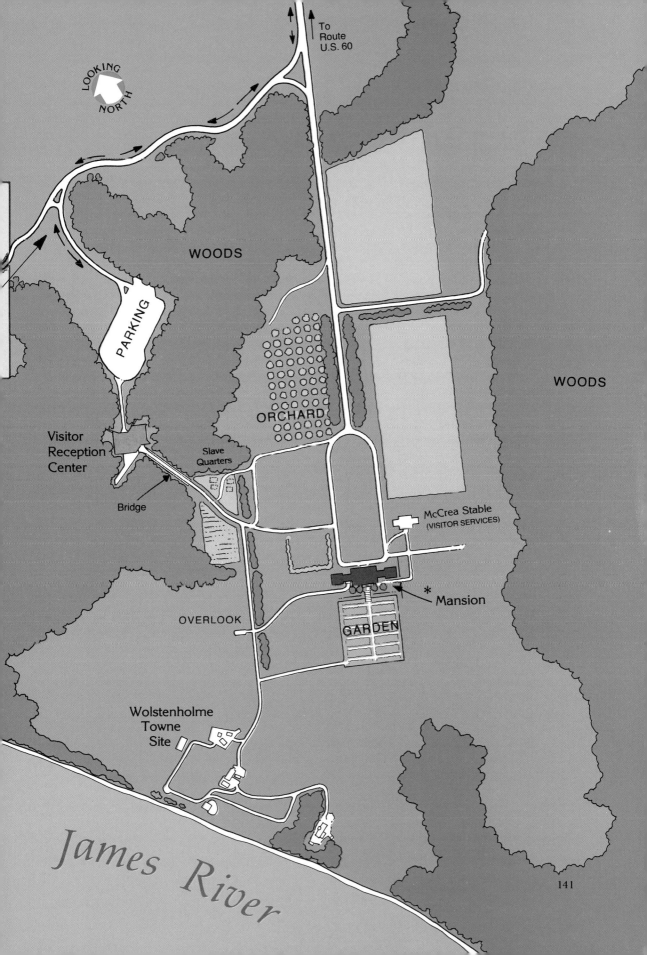

LOOKING NORTH

To Route U.S. 60

WOODS

PARKING

WOODS

ORCHARD

Visitor Reception Center

Slave Quarters

Bridge

McCrea Stable (VISITOR SERVICES)

* Mansion

OVERLOOK

GARDEN

Wolstenholme Towne Site

James River

141

* *Carter's Grove* T

come be called and to go by the name of Carter's Grove."

Carter Burwell contracted with David Minitree, a Williamsburg brickmason, to construct the masonry shell of the mansion for £115. He was so pleased with Minitree's work that he gave the artisan a bonus of twenty-five pounds. Burwell also paid Minitree for glazing 540 window-panes. Another Williamsburg craftsman, John Wheatley, directed the efforts of a number of slaves and journeymen carpenters who raised the timber framework of the floors and roof between 1751 and 1753. In 1752 Burwell paid for the passage to Virginia of Richard Baylis, an English joiner, and his family. Baylis and other skilled craftsmen were responsible for fashioning the magnificent woodwork at Carter's Grove.

The mansion today consists of five connected sections that stretch just over two hundred feet from end to end. The main house in the center was finished in 1755. The flanking eighteenth-century outbuildings—the kitchen at the eastern extremity and the laundry at the western end—are believed to predate the main house. The two hyphens that connect the kitchen and laundry to the central portion were constructed during 1930–1931. Carter's Grove is admired today for its superb brickwork, skillfully crafted interior wood-

work, and the sophistication of its original floor plan.

Carter Burwell died less than six months after his elegant new dwelling was completed. The estate passed to his five-year-old son Nathaniel, who came of age and to full authority over it in 1771.

Nathaniel Burwell skillfully managed the agricultural assets of his several tidewater plantations. Although he grew tobacco elsewhere, none of the "filthy weed" was produced at Carter's Grove. Some corn and wheat were harvested, however. In 1772 Burwell rebuilt and expanded his plantation mill, located several miles away. By damming a nearby creek, he created a millpond large enough to turn two sets of stones—one for corn, one for wheat. Burwell's account books show that many familiar Williamsburg residents, among them armorer James Anderson, wigmaker Edward Charlton, and tavern keeper Christiana Campbell, patronized his mill.

Other important cash crops included cider from the apples in Burwell's orchard, meat, and dairy products. Burwell also sold firewood and fodder to Williamsburg residents. In addition to field hands, Nathaniel Burwell's work force of black slaves included several craftsmen—a cooper, blacksmith, shoemaker, and carpenters—who supplied the needs of the plantation's agricultural operations.

Eight children were born to Nathaniel and Susannah Grymes Burwell, six of whom were living when she died in 1788. Nathaniel felt the loss of his beloved "Sukey" keenly, and he also needed someone to care for his brood and supervise his household. He soon persuaded Lucy Page Baylor, a widow with six children of her own, to marry him. The couple later had eight more children.

After his second marriage Nathaniel Burwell built another house in western Virginia and lived there almost exclusively after 1792, placing Carter's Grove in the hands of overseers. While his oldest son, Carter Burwell III, was born and died at Carter's Grove, he may actually have spent little of his adult life there. His only son, Philip Lewis Carter Burwell, sold the property in 1838, ending the ownership of Carter's Grove by five generations of Burwells.

During the nineteenth century the plantation was occupied by a series of owners and tenants who continued to farm the land much as the Burwells had done. In terms of its size and agricultural production, the "Grove farm," as it was called, remained one of the largest in the area.

Nineteenth-century residents of Carter's

Carter's Grove

Carter's Grove plantation is located on the James River eight miles southeast of Williamsburg. Completed in 1755, the handsome Georgian mansion was owned by five generations of the Burwell family.

Archaeological investigations have determined the site of the early seventeenth-century community of Wolstenholme Towne. The settlement was interrupted by an Indian uprising in 1622 when many of its inhabitants were killed or carried off.

Tours of the mansion emphasizing life there in the late 1930s occur daily when Carter's Grove is open to the public. Carpenters using eighteenth-century construction techniques are currently rebuilding the Carter's Grove slave quarter on its original site.

A Country Road (one way only from Williamsburg) connects Williamsburg and Carter's Grove.

Grove did make some changes to the house to accommodate their life styles. In the second half of the century they added a long Victorian veranda to the riverfront elevation and built a porch on the land side. A potbellied stove heated the front hall. The interior woodwork was painted, according to one outraged eyewitness, "in shrieking tones of red, white, blue, and —*mirabile dictu*—green!" Historians have speculated that it was done in connection with the 1881 centenary of the victory at Yorktown.

In 1928 Mr. and Mrs. Archibald M. McCrea purchased the property and, with the help of Richmond architect W. Duncan Lee, renovated and enlarged the house. The roof ridge of the main house was raised and dormer windows were added in order to make a livable third floor. The

Meet . . .
William Moody, Jr.

In addition to Carter's Grove plantation, Carter Burwell and his son Nathaniel owned several plantations, or "quarters" as they were called in the eighteenth century. In 1764 William Moody, Jr., began working for the Burwells as an overseer at Fouaces Quarter in nearby York County. Moody supervised the eight field hands that Burwell owned and had assigned to Fouaces. The overseer was responsible for most aspects of the day-to-day management of the farm. He had to know when to plant and when to harvest and how to get the most from every field hand and every acre.

Tobacco was the main crop at Fouaces. Wheat, corn, cider, pork, beef, mutton, wool, milk, and butter also brought in income. In lieu of a salary, Moody received two and one-half shares of the produce of the farm, an incentive for him to make the agricultural operations at Fouaces efficient and productive.

Sometimes an overseer was allowed to grow his own tobacco crop on his employer's land. Since Moody owned at least five slaves, he probably put them to work in his plot of tobacco. Like many other young overseers, Moody hoped to accumulate enough capital to acquire a farm of his own.

By 1750 four generations of Moodys had lived in York County for over a century. They were hard working, well-respected, civic-minded people who often served on juries and as estate appraisers.

In 1772 Moody married "Barbary," the widow of his friend Frederick Bryan for whose will Moody had acted as executor. Shortly thereafter Moody bought 175 acres of land in York County to which he soon added 150 more that he acquired from Burwell. By the late 1770s Moody had managed to establish himself as a landowning planter in his own right.

riverfront walls of the kitchen and laundry dependencies were set forward several feet and their roofs and second floors were remodeled accordingly. The original roof line is still visible among the old bricks in the west wall of the western dependency. Finally, the connectors were built to balance the whole composition and to provide protected access to the kitchen and laundry from both the front and rear rooms of the house.

Today the house and its furnishings, which date from the seventeenth, eighteenth, nineteenth, and twentieth centuries, are very much as they were left by Mrs. McCrea, who died in 1960. In her will, she stated a long-standing "hope and ambition" that the property might be maintained for the benefit of subsequent generations. Sealantic Fund, a philanthropic organization, purchased Carter's Grove from Mrs. McCrea's estate in 1963. In 1969 it was transferred by deed of gift to the Colonial Williamsburg Foundation, which today preserves Carter's Grove and its grounds for exhibition to the public.

In an effort to discover more of the eighteenth-century remains of Carter's Grove, the Colonial Williamsburg Foundation undertook extensive archaeological research supported in part by the National Geographic Society. Instead of eighteenth-century outbuildings, archaeological investigations uncovered the site of a major English settlement that dates from the early seventeenth century. Called Martin's Hundred, it was established by a company of English investors by 1620 but was interrupted by an Indian uprising in March 1622 when many of its inhabitants were killed or carried off. The sites of the early homes and the administrative center at Wolstenholme Towne slowly disappeared and remained "lost" until they were rediscovered in the 1970s.

Wolstenholme Towne was part of a much larger tract of some 21,500 acres called Martin's Hundred, whose name had been corrupted to "Merchant's Hundred"

by the end of the seventeenth century. Early in the eighteenth century "King" Carter purchased part of this land, which later descended to his grandson and became Carter's Grove.

Today, what remains of the riverfront site of Wolstenholme Towne lies below the

At eleven barrel-housed stations around the Wolstenholme Towne site, the voice of an archaeologist describes what the excavations revealed.

bluff on which the mansion house sits. The site is interpreted schematically. Its fort, store, houses, and dwellings are defined in a combination of reconstructed elements and linear definitions.

A "Country Road" links Williamsburg and Carter's Grove. Starting on South England Street, visitors may drive, cycle, or walk through woodland reminiscent of tidewater Virginia in the eighteenth century. The Country Road traverses marshes, tidal creeks, wooded hills, and open fields. It terminates at the Visitor Reception Center, where visitor services are available. Carter's Grove may also be reached by Route 60 East.

Meet . . .
Duncan Lee
and
Arthur Shurcliff

The radical changes in the fabric of Carter's Grove begun in 1928 were undertaken by the distinguished Virginia architect W. Duncan Lee (1884–1952). Nationally known as a specialist in colonial restoration and as a designer of fine Georgian residences, Lee some years earlier had expanded the governor's mansion in Richmond by the addition of an elegant oval dining room.

In the 1920s the "restoration" of a historic house to exactly the way it had been in a former, less comfortable era would have been unthinkable. To save such a house and maintain it as a museum might be justified, Lee wrote, "but if a person buys an old house, pays a lot of money for it, and intends to use it as a year-round home, he is not going to be satisfied to take his bath in a tin foot-tub and go to bed with a candle in one hand and a warming pan in the other." Instead, Lee and his clients had in mind a functional restoration that would be suitable for entertaining on a grand scale.

Lee saw his work at Carter's Grove—in descending order of importance—in four parts: enlarging the house, shoring up the structure, adding modern heat, plumbing, and electricity, and, finally, restoration that involved mainly the mansion's visible finishes.

The changes to the house were paralleled by extensive landscape revisions that Mr. and Mrs. McCrea asked Arthur Shurcliff to do at the same time. Shurcliff (1870–1957), a former apprentice to the father of American landscape architecture, Frederick Law Olmsted, Sr., opened the grand vista toward the river and was responsible for the venerable boxwood plantings that adorn the landside approach.

Coupled with the architectural changes made by Lee, Shurcliff's designs emphasized the mansion's land approach in order to make the greatest possible impression on guests arriving by car. In the eighteenth century, by contrast, the most formal facade and the most elaborately carved and paneled rooms were reserved for the riverfront side of the mansion.

Rather than undoing the Lee and Shurcliff changes, however unhistoric, Colonial Williamsburg has decided to preserve them with the same deference due an eighteenth-century artifact. The Colonial Revival period of the 1920s was vital to the history of historic preservation in America, extremely influential in American architecture, gardening, and decorative arts, and worth preserving in its own right. Without it, the rebirth of Williamsburg itself might never have come to pass.

Modern Accommodations

ALL visitors are invited and urged to go first to the **Visitor Center.** It is the gateway to Colonial Williamsburg and the first step of a journey in space and time.

A brief audiovisual presentation offers an exciting and informative montage of the many sights, sounds, activities, and personalities to be found during a visit to the Historic Area. Informational kiosks help visitors plan their stay, purchase tickets, and make reservations for lodging and dining.

Every visitor should see *Williamsburg— The Story of a Patriot,* a thirty-five-minute film that is projected continuously in twin theaters. The film, made by Paramount Pictures for Colonial Williamsburg, is a dramatic introduction to the history and significance of Williamsburg.

The Visitor Center bookstore offers a complete selection of titles relating to Colonial Williamsburg and the eighteenth century. Post cards, recordings, and slides are available; film and camera accessories are also sold here.

As visitors leave the Visitor Center, they will find buses waiting to take them directly to the Historic Area. Since streets in the Historic Area are closed to motor vehicles, visitors should leave their cars at the Visitor Center and ride the Colonial Williamsburg buses.

The **Group Arrivals Building** serves all adult and student group arrivals. Groups purchase tickets, receive orientation, and attend special educational programs in the Group Arrivals Building.

The Motor House, Williamsburg's largest and finest motor hotel, is perfect for visitors who prefer a casual atmosphere and informal lodgings furnished in the contemporary manner. Its suites and double and twin-bedded rooms have picture windows that frame views of The Motor House's wooded grounds.

The Motor House has pools, a complete children's playground, and badminton, ping-pong, and tetherball. Guests enjoy shuffleboard, horseshoe pitching, and a putting green and miniature golf course.

The two-story **Cascades** offers attractive contemporary suites.

Motor House and Cascades guests are invited to use the tennis courts and golf courses at the Inn and the Tazewell Fitness Center at the Lodge.

The **Motor House Cafeteria** is adjacent to The Motor House and the Visitor Center. A wide variety of popular dishes is available at reasonable prices. The Cafeteria

The Motor House reception building.

provides convenient and economical meals for visitors to Virginia's colonial capital.

The ***Cascades Restaurant,*** located on the grounds of The Motor House, specializes in favorites from the Chesapeake Bay country at breakfast, lunch, and dinner. The famous Hunt Breakfast buffet, Monday through Saturday, and the Sunday Hunt Brunch are outstanding. From the terrace, diners enjoy the beautiful wooded setting complete with waterfall.

The Cascades Meeting Center offers modern, well-maintained, completely equipped space for groups of any size. All meeting rooms contain the latest audiovisual equipment and training aids.

The ***Governor's Inn,*** located two blocks from the Historic Area and convenient to the Visitor Center, is ideal for economy minded visitors who want comfortable, informal surroundings. Governor's Inn guests may use all the sports facilities at the Williamsburg Inn.

The ***Williamsburg Inn*** is one of the nation's most distinguished hotels. The Inn is renowned for the excellence of its appointments, superb cuisine, and attentive service. The Inn has received the Mobil Travel Guide's highest rating, the prestigious Five-Star Award.

Convenient and economical meals are available in The Motor House Cafeteria.

The popular Hunt Breakfast at the Cascades.

The sports area at The Motor House is next to the pools.

Guests enjoy the gracious hospitality of the award-winning Williamsburg Inn, one of America's most distinguished hotels.

The Williamsburg Inn has welcomed hundreds of VIP guests. Among the many world figures who have enjoyed the cordial hospitality at the Inn are Queen Elizabeth and Prince Philip, the Emperor and Empress of Japan, and U. S. Presidents Harry S Truman, Dwight D. Eisenhower, Richard M. Nixon, Gerald Ford, and Ronald W. Reagan.

The Williamsburg Inn was the site of the 1983 Economic Summit of Industrialized Nations, hosted by President Reagan.

The fashionable hotels at West Virginia spas where the socially elite went in the nineteenth century to take the waters at hot or sulfurous springs inspired the architecture of the Williamsburg Inn. Its handsome white brick exterior harmonizes successfully with the colonial buildings in the Historic Area.

The furniture and interior decorations are in the Regency style that was popular early in the nineteenth century. The lobby, lounges, and guest rooms capture the quiet luxury of a Virginia country estate. Terraces overlooking the tranquil green countryside invite guests to pause for a moment of relaxation and reflection.

In the Regency Dining Room guests enjoy distinctive food and wines in an atmosphere of graceful elegance. The cosmopolitan cuisine is prepared under the direction of a European-trained chef.

Many colonial homes, taverns, and quarters located in the Historic Area are operated as guest facilities by the Inn.

The Clubhouse overlooks picturesque ponds that border the 18th green.

Lawn bowling at the Inn.

Eight courts and a tennis shop are adjacent to the Inn.

The Regency Dining Room at the Williamsburg Inn has long been renowned for its excellent cuisine.

Light food service and a wide selection of beverages are available in the Regency Lounge, where there is entertainment nightly. Tea is served daily in the East Lounge of the Inn.

Sports-minded Inn guests can choose from a variety of outdoor activities. A lawn bowling green and a croquet court invite participation in these ancient and genteel pastimes. A brochure that identifies measured jogging routes of varying distances is useful to those who prefer a more strenuous way to exercise.

Tennis enthusiasts will enjoy playing a set or two on the four Har-Tru or four all-weather courts adjacent to the east lawn. A tennis shop is located next to the courts.

The Inn offers a choice of two large swimming pools. Each has an attractive poolside area that is ideal for sunning and relaxing after a day of sightseeing or sports.

Two challenging golf courses have been laid out next to the Williamsburg Inn. The par 71, 18-hole championship Golden Horseshoe Course and the par 31, 9-hole executive-length Spotswood Course were both designed by Robert Trent Jones. A practice range, rental clubs, electric carts, and golf equipment are available. A resident professional and his staff are on duty.

The **Clubhouse** overlooking picturesque lakes that border the starting and finishing holes of both courses is the headquarters for golfers at Colonial Williamsburg. A lounge, complete golf shop, men's and women's sports clothing and furnishings, and spacious locker and dressing rooms are among the facilities available at the Clubhouse. Light meals and refreshments are offered in the Clubhouse Grill, and beverages are also served in the Golden Horseshoe Cocktail Lounge.

Located in the Historic Area are more than a score of colonial homes, taverns, and quarters that are operated as guest facilities by the Williamsburg Inn. The **Colonial Houses** range in size from larger taverns, such as Brick House Tavern, to the tiny Lightfoot Kitchen tucked away in a garden. Guests who stay in these colonial accommodations enjoy all of the conveniences and privileges of guests at the Inn itself.

Providence Hall offers deluxe parlor and bed-sitting rooms just adjacent to the Williamsburg Inn. The spacious rooms overlook the tennis courts and a beautiful natural wooded area complete with ponds and waterfowl. Guests enjoy all of the conveniences and privileges of guests at the Inn itself.

Providence Hall House was built about 1770 and later moved to this site. The re-

The Williamsburg Lodge, Conference Center, and Auditorium.

Seafood is a specialty in the Lodge Bay room.

Inn and Lodge guests relax around the pool.

stored residence is noted for its elegance, ambience, and location. The facilities at Providence Hall have been designed for small executive meetings or conferences and for social gatherings as well. The Inn furnishes all staff and services.

The **Williamsburg Lodge, Conference Center, and Auditorium,** just a few steps from the Historic Area, are directly across from the Golden Horseshoe Golf Course. Many of the rooms at the Lodge have private terraces or balconies that allow guests to enjoy the attractively landscaped grounds.

In addition to the recreational facilities of the Inn which the Lodge shares, its Tazewell Club Fitness Center features an indoor pool, exercise rooms, and a full service hair care salon.

The Lodge Bay Room offers its exciting food favorites for breakfast, lunch, and dinner. The Chesapeake Bay Feast on weekend evenings and Sunday brunch are featured. Seafood is a specialty of the Williamsburg Lodge.

The Coffee Shop offers sandwiches, light lunches, and delicious dinners. The handsome Garden Lounge is a gathering place for those seeking a respite from sightseeing or a busy round of meetings.

The Williamsburg Conference Center has meeting and banquet facilities for up to seven hundred persons.

Reproductions of many Williamsburg antiques are for sale at **Craft House,** which is located between the Inn and the Lodge. Included are furniture, glass, silver, brass, pewter, china, fabrics, wallpaper, paint, locks, iron, and lighting fixtures. Other items such as needlework, books, textiles, and jewelry are also available.

Craft House in Merchants Square is a second retail outlet for Williamsburg reproductions and other articles. The **Sign of the Rooster,** downstairs at Craft House in Merchants Square, features items inspired by the Abby Aldrich Rockefeller Folk Art Center collection.

Gift Shops are located in the lobbies of the Inn, Lodge, Motor House, and the Cascades. Each gift shop stocks a wide variety of special Williamsburg remembrances.

Craft House features enduring classics and new favorites from the Williamsburg Reproductions Program. Many of the reproductions have been arranged in room settings.

Books about Colonial Williamsburg

You can learn more about Colonial Williamsburg from the books published by the Colonial Williamsburg Foundation. The bookstore at the Visitor Center stocks a wide range of titles, including books on how-to Christmas decorations, plants and gardens, individual crafts, music, archaeology, the decorative arts, cookery, and publications for younger readers.

A Window on Williamsburg offers an intimate glimpse of the restored colonial capital of Virginia, its gardens and greens, its buildings great and small, its crafts, and its people.

Legacy from the Past illustrates in full color the 88 original eighteenth- and early nineteenth-century buildings in or near the Historic Area of Williamsburg.

The Eighteenth-Century Houses of Williamsburg provides historical backgrounds plus drawings, elevations, and details of Williamsburg's original eighteenth-century houses that range from the modest to the grand.

The Governor's Palace focuses on the elegant and imposing Virginia residence of the king's representative and the exquisite decorative arts objects that it contains.

The Crafts of Williamsburg celebrates the artisans of eighteenth-century Williamsburg and their contemporary counterparts. Today more than 100 men and women ply over 30 trades much like the kinds that were practiced in Virginia's colonial capital in the years before the American Revolution.

The Gardens of Williamsburg evokes the spirit of each season in this "green country town" where more than 100 gardens and several broad greens are alive with Nature's colors and textures.

The Williamsburg Cookbook contains 185 traditional and contemporary recipes from Colonial Williamsburg's famed taverns and dining places.

Favorite Meals from Williamsburg: A Menu Cookbook features 30 exciting menus composed of over 200 popular recipes from Colonial Williamsburg's talented chefs.

A Williamsburg Christmas captures the excitement of the festive holiday season in Williamsburg. It is truly an adventure into the world of Christmas past, a world that may still be enjoyed in this special town today.

Colonial Williamsburg by Philip Kopper, published by Harry N. Abrams, Inc., is a comprehensive look at Virginia's former colonial capital.

For a complete list of Colonial Williamsburg publications, write to:

Colonial Williamsburg
P.O. Box CH
Williamsburg, Virginia 23187

Index

The chief descriptive entry for each building is indicated by page numbers in **boldface** type; *identifies original buildings.

GIFTS and BEQUESTS

WHILE admission tickets purchased by our visitors provide one major source of funds needed to support the educational and museum programs at Colonial Williamsburg, the Foundation needs and encourages gifts and bequests from all Americans who believe in the special Williamsburg experience.

Gifts to the Colonial Williamsburg Fund make possible the research, preservation, and maintenance of the historic buildings and grounds, interpretation of the exhibition buildings and crafts, publication of manuscripts and other scholarly works, production of audiovisual materials, and conservation of the collections of period objects and works of art.

Gifts and bequests may be made to the Colonial Williamsburg Fund in the form of cash or securities. Gifts may also be placed in trust, the donor retaining the right to receive the trust income during the remainder of his life. Gifts of objects and contributions restricted for projects of special interest to the donor are also an important part of the public's support for Colonial Williamsburg.

All contributions made to the Colonial Williamsburg Fund are tax deductible, as provided by law. Friends interested in discussing gifts to Colonial Williamsburg are encouraged to write the Director of Development, The Colonial Williamsburg Foundation, Williamsburg, Virginia 23187.